Claptrap

Claptrap

a comedy
by
Tom Wood

SIMON & PIERRE
A MEMBER OF THE DUNDURN GROUP
TORONTO · OXFORD

Simon & Pierre
A Member of the Dundurn Group

Editor: Marc Côté
Copyeditor: Barry Jowett
Designer: Scott Reid
Printer: Transcontinental Printing Inc.

Canadian Cataloguing in Publication Data
Wood, Tom, 1950-
        Claptrap
A play.

ISBN 0-88924-279-8

I. Title

PS8595.06392C52 1998   C812'.54   C98-930811-1
PR9199.3.W66C52 1998

1 2 3 4 5   02 01 00 99 98

THE CANADA COUNCIL | LE CONSEIL DES ARTS
FOR THE ARTS | DU CANADA
SINCE 1957 | DEPUIS 1957

We acknowledge the support of the **Canada Council for the Arts** for our publishing program. We also acknowledge the support of the **Ontario Arts Council** and the **Book Publishing Industry Development Program** of the **Department of Canadian Heritage.**

Care has been taken to trace the ownership of copyright material used in this book. The author and the publisher welcome any information enabling them to rectify any references or credit in subsequent editions.

Printed and bound in Canada.

 Printed on recycled paper.
website: www.dundurn.com

Simon & Pierre   Simon & Pierre   Simon & Pierre
8 Market Street   73 Lime Walk   250 Sonwil Drive
Suite 200   Headington, Oxford   Buffalo, NY
Toronto, Ontario, Canada   England   U.S.A. 14225
M5E 1M6   OX3 7AD

Acknowledgements

Thanks to The Canada Council for the Arts for their great support in allowing me to embark on this venture in the first place, and to Joan Chalmers and Barbra Amesbury for giving generous support to the production.

Thanks also to the Canadian Stage Company for the commission and development, and to the National Arts Centre and the Manitoba Theatre Centre for their added developmental support.

Thanks to the Canadian Stage Company and the National Arts Centre for deciding to co-produce the premiere.

I am indebted also to Don Horsburgh, Katherine Kaszas, Iris Turcott, Ray Salverda and Chris Abraham for all their hard work, inspiration, and encouragement, and to Rina Fraticelli and David McIlwraith for first believing in this play and laughing out loud.

Thanks to the National Arts Centre Production Department: props, costumes, carpenters, and technicians, for their dedication and brilliance on this production.

Thanks also to Maria Vacratsis, Brian Tree, Lindsay Leese, Brenda Robins, Michael Lamport, Michael Hanrahan, Sara Evans, Randy Read, Marylin Michener, Shadi Mogadime, Marianne Copithorne, Robert Persichini, Jamie Robinson, Jeff Douglas, Lorne Kennedy, Nicola Cavendish, Janet Wright, Caleb Marshall, Christine Oddy, Tim French, John Stead, Kevin Lamotte, Thom Payne, Bona Duncan, and Jennifer Strahl.

For Bob, Candy, and Leslie

The Original Cast
(in alphabetical order)

Claptrap was first produced by the National Arts Centre English Theatre and The Canadian Stage Company. It opened February 5, 1998, at the National Arts Centre Theatre in Ottawa, with the folowing cast:

Carol Quill/Patsy	**Nicola Cavendish**
Various Roles	**Paul Fauteux**
Dirk Hart/Various Roles	**Roger Honeywell**
Claire Ford	**Lisa Horner**
Antony Manley-Dunn	**Lorne Kennedy**
Ben Palmer	**Caleb Marshall**
Various Roles	**Christine Oddy**
Julia Hudson	**Lucy Peacock**
Simon Webber-Douglas	**Tom Wood**
Patricia (Trish) Lovell	**Janet Wright**
Stage Manager	**Thom Payne**
Assistant Stage Manager	**Bona Duncan**
Apprentice Stage Manager	**Jennifer Strahl**
Directed by	**Bob Baker**
Set and Costume design by	**Leslie Frankish**
Lighting design by	**Kevin Lamotte**
Music composed by	**Don Horsburgh**

The Toronto Cast

Claptrap was revised and moved to Toronto, where it was produced by the Canadian Stage Company and the National Arts Centre English Theatre. It opened April 9, 1998, at the Bluma Appel Theatre of the St. Lawrence Centre for the Arts, with the following cast:

Carol Quill/Patsy	**Nicola Cavendish**
Various Roles	**Paul Fauteux**
Dirk Hart/Various Roles	**Roger Honeywell**
Claire Ford	**Lisa Horner**
Antony Manley-Dunn	**Lorne Kennedy**
Patricia (Trish) Lovell	**Judy Marshak**
Ben Palmer	**Caleb Marshall**
Various Roles	**Christine Oddy**
Julia Hudson	**Lucy Peacock**
Simon Webber-Douglas	**Tom Wood**
Stage Manager	**Thom Payne**
Assistant Stage Manager	**Bona Duncan**
Apprentice Stage Manager	**Jennifer Strahl**
Directed by	**Bob Baker**
Set and Costume design by	**Leslie Frankish**
Lighting design by	**Kevin Lamotte**
Music composed by	**Don Horsburgh**

Dramatis Personae

Julia Hudson
Actress, late 30's, divorced.
Antony Manley-Dunn
An Artistic Director, British, 40's. A monster.
Simon Webber-Douglas
A Canadian born, British trained Actor.
Patricia (Trish) Lovell
Actress, 50's, big heart, heavy drinker.
Ben Palmer
Recent theatre school graduate, 20's, keen.
Claire Ford
A dancer and actress. 20's. Ambitious.
Carol Quill
Stage manager, late 30's. Large and devoted to ANTONY.
Patsy
A very short apprentice. Keen. Aspiring actress.
Dirk Hart
Television Personality, hunky, white toothed, American.

Spud & Bud
Crew guys. Burley, large, biker-type dudes.
Lloyd Garrick
Plays Clive, a Bengal Lancer in The Raj.
Jeremy Atkins-Austin
Plays Pantilous in Pantilous in Crete. *Old, grand, and British.*
Gary Wolfe
Plays Alphonse in Frozen Wheat. *From the Method School.*

Claptrap takes place during the 36ᵗʰ season of the *Ibsen Summer Festival* in Oslo, Ontario. The company has 55 members, and the Festival has three performing spaces. We, however, are only concerned with the Main Stage.

 The Festival is in the middle of its repertory season: *Virtue Slandered* (a Restoration play), *The Raj* (a Gilbert and Sullivan (type) musical), *Pantilous In Crete* (a Greek Tragedy) and *Frozen*

Wheat (a Canadian Drama) have already opened. *The Twins*, a Commedia Dell'Arte play, is in technical rehearsal and an unnamed Ibsen (the late season opener) will begin rehearsal in three weeks.

ACT ONE

Scene One — On Stage.
Technical rehearsal for *The Twins*. Friday Afternoon, July.
Scene Two — Backstage, that same evening, at a performance of *Virtue Slandered*.
Scene Three — Saturday Afternoon. Simultaneously: (1) On Stage/Backstage at a performance of *The Raj*. (2) In the Janitor's Closet. (3) In the rehearsal hall.

ACT TWO

Scene One — Saturday night. Backstage after a performance of *Pantilous in Crete*.
Scene Two — A week later. Onstage rehearsal for *The Twins*.
Scene Three — Eleven p.m., Saturday. Onstage on the set of *The Twins*.
Scene Four — Time Passage Montage. Backstage during performances and at the hospital.
Scene Five — Backstage on opening night of *The Twins*.
Scene Six — Onstage on opening night of *The Twins*.

Please note: Normal dialogue is printed in this type face, while all lines from the plays within the play, are printed in this type face.

Act One, Prologue

[Spotlight up on JULIA *as she stands on the apron of the stage, shielding her eyes. She peers out into a darkened theatre.]*

JULIA ...yes ... yes, Antony. I ... *(pause)* Well, this one's very short. *(pause)* Yes, I realize you only wanted the one audition speech but... *(subtly checks her watch)*...I do get ten minutes, and by my calculations, I still have five... so if I hurry I... *(pause)* Thank you. Thank you, Antony. *(clearing throat)* This is from Silverati's *The Twins.* Beatrice, disguised as her twin brother, is captured by pirates and sold to the Maestro Spavento, villainous owner of a troupe of travelling players. She... What? *(pause)* Oh, of course you should know the plot, you're directing it next season. *(catching herself)* I mean...I've heard. Word has it, the Festival's doing a Commedia. This Commedia. And I'd... I'd kill to play Beatrice. It's one of those roles that only comes along... *(pause)* Oh. Already cast. *(pause)* Who's um...? *(pause)* Ah! *(pause)* No. No I don't know her. But I'm sure she'll be great. Great role. Well...here we go anyway. Beatrice after her first disastrous rehearsal with the Maestro. *(taking a second, then launching in beautifully.)*

"Invention?!" He cuffs me on the cheek, and bids me: "look to my invention!" Ye Gods! Is it not invention enough that I, to the world, present myself as Orazio, my brother, without... *(jolts)* Pardon? *(pause)* "Or-a-ZEE-oh?" Ah. Thank you Antony. Or-a-ZEE-oh, of course.

"Invention?!" He cuffs me on the cheek, and bids me: "look to my invention!" Ye Gods! Is it not invention enough that I, to the world, present myself as OraZEEo, my brother, without I must portray Lelio the lover besides. And all under the cruel scrutiny of this tyrant, this devil, who with the back of his hand, compels me to extemporize. Constrained invention! Laborious levity! Impossible opposites!! Till now did I fancy the Commedia a magical game whose only precept was innocent play. The very boards, imagination's nursery. Each player a free spirit and joyful child. His genius nothing more nor less than childhood regained at will. *(pause)* His genius nothing more nor less than childhood regained at will...? *(pause)*

I've dried. Sorry, Antony. One second, I've got the script here in my ... *(she scoots out of the spotlight)* This audition means so much to me, my brain won't shut up. You know that actor's brain thing. Always observing, always criticising. Always at the wrong moment. *(back in light)* Nothing's sacred. *(using the light to find the script)* I mean when Patrick and I broke up for God's sake! I was crying and screaming at him — "how could you after I've sacrificed my career to move out here!" — and at the same time my actor's brain is saying: "Sacrificed your career? Who wrote this?" And while I'm screaming "Patrick, I'm leaving you!" that little part of my brain is screaming back: "Julia, don't open your mouth so wide!" Then I'm waiting for the elevator, sobbing my guts out in the hall, and it's whispering... "Remember this, Julia... This is what your heart breaking feels like." *(pause)* Here it is. Too late. Sorry. Thank you. *(leaves, comes back)* Antony, I'm desperate to come back to the Festival. I need to do the classics again. I don't care how I'm cast. I really...I just... *(pause)* Anyway, thank you. Thank you for seeing me. *(pause)* Antony? *(looking out into the void)* Antony? Mr Manley-Dunn? [*Realizing that* ANTONY *has left the auditorium, she begins to exit. Blackout. In the darkness we hear:*]

SIMON   *(as Maestro)* Stop! Halt! Desist!

Scene One

[*Lights up, full and brilliant, on the courtyard of an Italian inn. A technical dress rehearsal of* The Twins. *A two-storey inn with sweeping staircase is stage right and a church with double doors, stage left. A small platform sits downstage. Across it is strung a crude painted curtain. Theatrical props, banners, and a very large wicker basket are strewn about the courtyard. A troupe of masked Commedia actors are in the midst of rehearsing a very animated song and dance. A black crow of a man (the Maestro) paces off to the side, barking orders. Two peasants watch the spectacle.*]

ALL   *(singing)* Fallder all dee, Fallder all dee day. Pish mimsy tiddle awaaaay…

SIMON   Useless! Bloody useless!

ALL   *(singing continued)* With a high thee-dum dum do-diddle diddle…

SIMON   *(scattering peasants)* Aside!

ALL   *(cont'd)* …dipsy-day diddly-die doh do-oh……

[TRISH *plays the Commedia actress Lucille, a member of the Maestro's troupe, who at this point is playing Smeraldina, a comic maid (masked).* DIRK *plays the actor Giro, who is playing Arlecchino, a masked clown.* CLAIRE *plays Beatrice, who, in disguise as her twin brother Orazio, is assaying the role of Lelio the lover (masked).*]

SIMON   Stop, I say!

[TRISH *and* DIRK *stop dancing, but* CLAIRE *continues.* SIMON *rushes to the platform and grabs* CLAIRE, *throwing her down front.*]

SIMON   This rubbish will never do! You dance like some great galumphing girl!

CLAIRE	*(as Beatrice/Orazio, removing her mask)* Forgive me Maestro. T'will improve I swear…
SIMON	Silence! *(he hits her)* Begin again. And I warn you, boy. Look to your invention.

> [CLAIRE *runs around behind the curtain on the platform.* SIMON *begins to chase after her.*]

SIMON	OraZEEo, hold!
TRISH	*(as Lucille, removing her mask, blocking the Maestro's way)* I will fetch the lad, sir.
DIRK	*(as Giro, removing his mask)* 'Twas not the boy's intent to displease, Maestro.
SIMON	*(pushing DIRK down)* Aside, fool! OraZEEo, in front I say!

> [TRISH, DIRK, *and* SIMON *disappear behind the curtain as* CLAIRE *comes out front of it. She begins removing her "Lelio" costume.*]

CLAIRE	*(aside, as Beatrice)* By heavens! I am undone if he do perceive I am not all the man I present.
SIMON	*(from off)* OraZEEo!!
CLAIRE	And now a woman's tears!
TRISH	*(head through curtains)* The Maestro grows marvellous mad.
CLAIRE	"Invention?!" He cuffs me on the cheek, and bids me: "Look to my invention!" Ye Gods! Is it not invention enough that I, to the world, present myself as OrEEazo, my brother, without I must portray Lelio the lover besides. And all under the cruel scrutiny of this tyrant, this devil, who with the back of his hand, compels me to extemporize.
SIMON	*(pushing DIRK through curtains, whip raised)* Where be that effeminate layabout!?
TRISH	*(following, pulling on his sleeve)* The lad is not schooled in our ways of extemporaneous invention!
SIMON	My whip shall be his tutor!
TRISH	Maestro …
SIMON	*(turns, grabs TRISH roughly)* Out front, hussy! You pamper this dandy.

> [*As the Maestro (*SIMON*) turns on Lucille (*TRISH*),*

    Beatrice/Orazio (CLAIRE) *picks up a lute and raises it
    to smash the Maestro on the head. Giro* (DIRK) *is
    meant to stop this at the last second but has forgotten
    and the lute comes down swiftly and with a loud
    thump on* SIMON*'s head. All actors drop character.*]

SIMON   Oufff!

CAROL   *(voice over speaker)* Stop, please!

CLAIRE   Tsk! Dirk!

DIRK   Yo, time out! *(to* CLAIRE*)* What? What was that?

SIMON   Not to fuss.

CLAIRE   *(fed up)* Dirk, like ya havta grab the guitar an' that.

SIMON   I'm right as rain, really.

DIRK   I don't think so, babe.

SIMON   *(to* TRISH*)* Am I bleeding?

CLAIRE   *(to* DIRK*)* Are you kidding?

SIMON   *(to* TRISH, *having removed his wig)* Stitches, d'you
    think?

CLAIRE   *(to* DIRK*)* That's like the bit right? You grab the guitar
    before I hit him.

DIRK   I know the bit. *(to* CAROL *in the control booth)* But I
    go ta grab it, it's not there.

CLAIRE   It was there. Okay! I *know* the bit. Like I was a
    dancer, alright!

DIRK   An' you've been on Broadway how many times, babe?

CLAIRE   You know, none…but… *(tears beginning)* Geeze, Dirk.
    [CLAIRE *begins to cry and* DIRK *comforts her, in a
    touchy feely way.*]

CAROL   *(v.o.)* Let's keep moving, shall we.
    [DIRK *and* CLAIRE *don't seem to hear.*]

SIMON   *(to* TRISH, *about* DIRK*)* Vulgar exhibitionist.

CAROL   *(v.o.)* Mr Hart?! Miss Ford?!

SIMON   He's got no sense of place.

CLAIRE   Dirk, honey, don't. *(giggling)*

TRISH   Simon, you're drooling.

SIMON   Ohff, you're no one to speak.

TRISH   Don't start.

SIMON   Oh no, but you can haul Hart off into the sack…

TRISH   Just breaking the ice.

SIMON	Who do you think you are? The bloody Ibsen Festival welcome wagon. *(coughs)*
CAROL	*(v.o.)* Let's pick it up, please. From Simon's line …
SIMON	*(to* TRISH*)* Do you find it dry?
CAROL	*(v.o.)* "and Fashion it with some wit."
DIRK	What, we're not gonna take that bit again?
SIMON	It's like the Sahara in here.
CAROL	Antony promises to rehearse it later, Mr Hart.
DIRK	I tell ya Tony, this ain't the way we get things done in the States.
JULIA	Do you believe that guy?
TRISH	Julia.
JULIA	Well…
TRISH	Keep your trap shut, hon.
DIRK	*(to booth)* Come on pal, let's go hard or go home, okay?
SIMON	*(close to wings to someone off)* Wa-tah?
CAROL	{ Mr Webber-Douglas?
SIMON	{ Wa…tah.
SIMON	Sorry?
CAROL	When you're ready.
SIMON	Not from the tap. *(to* TRISH*)* Where from?
TRISH	"Fashion it with some wit."
SIMON	Oh yes of course. *(off)* And my lozenges. Patsy!
DIRK	*(snapping fingers at* SIMON*)* Hit it, pops.
SIMON	*(extremely jovial)* Ha ha. Pops! Ha ha.
DIRK	In my lifetime!
SIMON	*(with false affection)* Oh, you Americans! Ah!
DIRK	*(yelling)* Put some hair on it!
SIMON	*(as the Maestro)* Fashion shit with some wip!
	[*Alarmed,* SIMON *backs into a potted tree, which becomes entangled in his costume. It trails behind him.*]
SIMON	Oh dear, I….
CAROL	*(v.o.)* Keep moving!
SIMON	But, but… *(disentangles it from his costume)*
CAROL	*(v.o.)* Patsy will deal with it later. Ms Ford.
	[SIMON *exits upstage of the painted curtain on the*

mini-stage. CLAIRE *(as Beatrice/Orazio) hurriedly begins gathering together some belongings and stuffing them into a leather bag.*]

CLAIRE   Giro, adieu.

DIRK   Nay, OraziOH, hold off your flight.
   (grabbing CLAIRE*'s arm)*

CLAIRE   *(dropping character)* Ouch, Dirk!

DIRK   Be not so rash.

CLAIRE   *(about arm)* That is, like, a hickie now!

DIRK   There is no 'scaping the Maestro's net.

CLAIRE   I am not his dancing dog!

DIRK   Even though our circumstance seems worse than slavery, we may stand some chance of betterment if the Duke do favour our play.

CLAIRE   Play! A strange word when he may make such toil of it.

DIRK   *(aside, with much hair and teeth acting)*
   What unnatural enchantment is it possesses me to love this lad? *(pause)* Hey Tony, didn't we green-light a tune here in my closeup…

CAROL   *(v.o.)* Mr Hart, there *is* underscoring in that particular "aside"…

DIRK   No kidding.

CAROL   *(v.o.)* But… you don't say it for two more pages. Miss Ford, would you put us back please.

CLAIRE   Sure. Play! A strange word when he may make such toil of it.

DIRK   Stay and together we shall devise some plot 'gainst the Maestro.

CLAIRE   I would sure run mad, Giro, were I strung here longer, puppet to this ogre.

DIRK   Then go, OraziOH. But I vow I will search you out.

CLAIRE   I am not OrEEazo, friend.

DIRK   Not OriazOH?

SIMON   Begin, wench!

TRISH   *(fierce whisper)* Enter OraZEEo!

DIRK   By what name might I find thee out?

CLAIRE   My family are the Rasponis of Turin.

SIMON   OraZEEo!!

CLAIRE   OrEEazo is…or was, my darling brother. My twin. I
          am…

          [TRISH, *as Lucille, sticks her arm between the
          curtains, and in one yank pulls* CLAIRE *through them
          and upstage with her.* DIRK *is left alone downstage.*]

TRISH   *(off, without missing a beat)* Late!

DIRK   ⎰ *(looking around, lost and out of character)*
          ⎱ What the fff…?

TRISH   *(off)* Ah Lelio, at last. What say you?

DIRK   ⎰ Shit. Um…

TRISH   ⎱ No words of love?

DIRK   ⎰ Oh yeah! *(grabs pirate-costume pieces)* Zounds! *(moves
          ⎱ to trapdoor in the stage floor and opens it)*

TRISH   No song? Oh La! I'll fetch my lute. *(reaching her hand
            back through the curtain)*

DIRK   ⎰ Desperation has hatched in me a plot. *(he walks down
TRISH   ⎱ the trap, leaving the door open)*
            My lovely little lute… *(gestures behind her for* DIRK *to
            hand her the prop)*…so we may … My lute…? So we
            may… *(backing up, more frantic gesturing)* … lilt a
            luscious lay… *(almost falling down open trap)* Oohh
            shit!

          [*All drop character.*]

CAROL   *(v.o.)* Stop, please.

JULIA   Trish?!

TRISH   Oh, Jesus.

JULIA   You okay?

TRISH   I'll live.

JULIA   I wonder who he'll blame it on this time?

DIRK   *(from somewhere in the trap room)* Dresser!

JULIA   Not Patsy!

SIMON   Is it me? *(appearing from behind curtain)* Did I get
          my cue?

DIRK   Dresser!

JULIA   Three days to previews and he can't even…

TRISH   Let it go.

JULIA   Someone's gonna get hurt.

SIMON   *(to* TRISH*)* Have I gone awry?

JULIA	*(strongly to* TRISH*)* Why doesn't Tony do something!
SIMON	*(to booth)* Carol?
TRISH	What did I tell you?!
JULIA	Well, he's the director!
TRISH	Julia!
SIMON	Sorry, Tony. I…
TRISH	Simon.
SIMON	Mmm?
TRISH	Shut up.
SIMON	Eh?
TRISH	It wasn't you. *(indicates* DIRK, *who's still down the trap)*
SIMON	Again? How absolutely nervous-making.
CAROL	*(v.o.)* We'll have to set back on that, ladies and gentlemen.
SIMON	Terrifying really.
JULIA	*(to booth)* Excuse me, Antony, but I think it's…
TRISH	*Julia!*
CLAIRE	*(calling down trap)* Dirk, honey. Ya like, totally skipped!
TRISH	*(dragging* JULIA *downstage)* What did you promise me?
JULIA	But I'm not…
TRISH	What did you promise?
JULIA	"Never argue with Tony."
TRISH	And?
JULIA	"Never answer back."
TRISH	And never ever make any suggestions. You don't know how crazy he's gotten.
JULIA	Well, Dirk's gonna kill this play! Not to mention one of us. He's gotta…
TRISH	Tony's not gonna risk his ticket to Broadway by pissing off his star. You worked hard to get back here, Jule. Don't blow it.

[PATSY *enters with water and lozenges. She is an extremely short apprentice stage manager.*]

PATSY	Mr. Webber-Douglas.
SIMON	Oh, Patsy. Ta. I'm absolutely parched.
PATSY	It's murder on your *(indicating throat)* instrument. Right? That's what the voice-coach calls it.

Instrument. I'm always working on mine. Hoping one day I might get the chance to be out here.

DIRK   *(from backstage)* Dresser!!

PATSY   *(fear)* Oh, geeze.

[PATSY *begins to drag the misplaced tree, left.*]

DIRK   *(entering from the "inn door" in complete disarray but giving it his best shot)* Aguzzio, the pirate, at your service!

CAROL   *(v.o.)* Thank you, Mr Hart...

DIRK   Prepare to pay your debt, dog...

CAROL   Mr Hart ...

DIRK   ...with your life...

CAROL   ...we've stopped!!

DIRK   Oh, for Chrissake. I'm bustin my friggin' hump here trying keep with the program an' you've "stopped?" An' where the hell's that goddammed dresser!

PATSY   I'm...I'm right here, Mr Hart.

DIRK   *(coming down stairs, to* PATSY*)* What are ya, *short* on brains as well?!

[PATSY'*s lip begins to quiver and she starts to cry..* TRISH *crosses to* PATSY.]

TRISH   Give it a rest, Dirk.

DIRK   What?

CLAIRE   Dirk ...

DIRK   Hey, Tony!

CLAIRE   ...honey, ya skipped again...

DIRK   Buddy!

CLAIRE   ... like two whole pages...

DIRK   Claire, babe. Cool it! I gotta situation here, okay? Tony!?

CAROL   *(v.o.)* Antony's just stepped out of the booth, Mr Hart.

DIRK   Terrific! I'm up to my balls in incompetence down here and the director's taking a dump!

CLAIRE   *(raising her hand)* Then, like, do I have time to call my agent, an' that?

DIRK   This concerns you, babe. Listen up, people. I got one hellava quick change down there, *(indicating the trap room)* and what do you know, no dresser! *Why* am I not surprised!

CAROL   *(v.o.)* Mr Hart, Patsy was on her way to the quick-change booth when…

DIRK   *(pause)* What?! *(pause)* I'm aging here!

JULIA   When you cut half the scene!

DIRK   *(stares at her for a furious second)* An' who's harebrained idea was it to put three thousand buttons on this faggy little vest. "Quick-change." Get it? "*Quick-change!*" *(pulls off his vest, tosses it at* PATSY*)* Okay!? Nuff said!?

[PATSY *exits offstage left, dragging the tree as:*]

JULIA   No, Dirk. Not quite.

DIRK   *(to Carol)* And somebody's gotta do something about this candy-assed stair railing. It's one bitch of a drop onto that cement floor.

CAROL   *(v.o.)* I'll send Spud round to have a look. Let's press on, please. If we could pick it up from your exit, Mr Hart.

DIRK   I'm all over it! *(all pumped)* Full-court press, people!

JULIA   Carol? What about the trap?

CAROL   *(v.o.)* Oh, yes. Mr Hart?

DIRK   Yo!

CAROL   *(v.o.)* This time around if you wouldn't mind … closing the *trap door* behind you.

CLAIRE   Oh yah, ha ha ha, right, Dirk. Ya left it open again.

DIRK   *(glaring at her)* What!?

CLAIRE   The trap. Ya forgot ta… well, you know "the trap?" That little door there in the floor? You forgot…

DIRK   *(exploding)* I know what a trap door is, babe! But what I can't figger out is how I'm sapposed ta remember a million pissy little details *and* carry this entire show on my back at the same time! Okay!?

JULIA   You *have* to close the trap, Dirk, or someone's going to get hurt.

DIRK   Well, why can't Claire…

JULIA   Claire doesn't get over there soon enough. And Trish isn't supposed to know anything about it. It's gotta be you, Dirk. Look, perhaps if you were to think of why you're going down there in the first place?

DIRK   Fffff. To change my gear.

JULIA   But in the play? This trap leads to the "sewer." Right?

DIRK   Well, duh.

JULIA   And the sewer has a passage to the *(pointing)* inn.

DIRK   I hear ya.

JULIA   And you're disguising yourself as Aguzzio the Pirate to… ?

DIRK   …scare the shit out of pops here.

JULIA   Great. But you see… "*they*" *(indicating audience)* have to know that. And you…you get to tell them.

[ANTONY *enters the auditorium. He prowls down the aisle to the apron of the stage.*]

DIRK   I do?

JULIA   Yes. It's all in the speech you…we skipped. So if you think of it as a great big secret between you and them…

DIRK   Sounds like a plan.

[*The cast, except* JULIA *and* DIRK, *have spotted* ANTONY *walking up the aisle. They begin to back away.*]

JULIA   And you don't want anyone to know that you've gone so…you close the trap when you ek… *(seeing* ANTONY, *she freezes dead)*…sit.

ANTONY Directing, are we now, Miss Hudson?

JULIA   Sorry, Antony. I was just thinking I could help…

ANTONY *(rushing up the stairs to the stage)* Well, you weren't actually thinking at all, were you? That's the trouble really, absence of any bloody thought, and it reads, you realize. It reads to the sodding back of the stalls!

JULIA   It's just that this trap…

ANTONY Bloody Bossy Betty, as ever! One hoped that banishment to the regionals would have broken your busybody tendencies. But utter disappointment, you see.

JULIA   *(stepping forward)* Antony, it's danger…

ANTONY Don't move! We're trying to light you, aren't we. Positions, please! *(to booth)* Carol, love? Has that

	infuriating dwarf girl, that Taffy or…or Sassy — whatever… returned with my sandwich?
CAROL	*(v.o.)* Yes, Antony. *Patsy's* just left your lunch up here in the booth.
ANTONY	Well, run it down, would you. I'm feeling peckish. And Simon…
ANTONY ⌈	…darling.
SIMON ⌊	…darling. (SIMON *finishes* ANTONY*'s sentences*)
ANTONY	P. A. C. E.! There, now I've spelled it out for you…
ANTONY ⌈	… haven't…
SIMON ⌊	… haven't…
SIMON	Ah! You have, yes. Thank you, Antony old mean/man. Pace.
ANTONY	*The Twins* is an Italian…
ANTONY ⌈	Comedy.
SIMON ⌊	Comedy.
ANTONY	"La Commedia." Everyone's a bit droopy round …
ANTONY ⌈	…the edges.
SIMON ⌊	…the edges.
ANTONY	Sorry, but there we are. Bit…
ANTONY ⌈	…knackered.
SIMON ⌊	…knackered.
ANTONY	Oh, sod off,…
ANTONY ⌈	Simon.
SIMON ⌊	Simon.
SIMON	Ha ha ha ha.
DIRK	Say pal…
ANTONY	Except of course for you, Dirky.
	[DIRK *begins to swagger*]
ANTONY	Please! Maintain your positions! *(catching himself, suddenly solicitous)* They're setting the lights, you see. Bothersome but essential. Illuminate that darling phisog. Lovely American energy, this. Ben, you lurking? Benjamin, love?
BEN	*(entering from wings)* Yes, sir. I'm here.
ANTONY	Ah, young Master Palmer. Kiss, kiss. You keep your eyes on Dirk here and you'll learn something. In fact, you could all *pick up* a great whacking lot from Dirk.

TRISH	I can vouch for that.
ANTONY	Patricia? Something you'd like to share with us?
TRISH	Not any more. Thanks to modern pharmaceuticals.
ANTONY	*(confused)* What? Yes, well... *(to* BEN*)* Clever angel! Lovely loose pelvic work on that entrance. But next go 'round, do give me the "naked essence" of that subtle phrase, "Take on." "Take on the livery..." What is the line?
BEN	"She has, I suspect, taken on the livery of a man, and looks the mirror of myself..."
ANTONY	Tell me, what connotation does the word "livery" summon up for you, my boy?
BEN	Well, sir, I was using the idea of *horses*? I believe my character's objective is...
ANTONY	Horses. Lovely. You know, *I* see a great muscular servant; stripped and sweating. Bent over an anvil, abutting a raging fire. Torn leather apron... leather, *livery*, lubricate, and so on. Just free yourself up. Are those breaches binding, lad?
BEN	*(pause)* No.
	[CLAIRE *sniggers.*]
ANTONY	Freeze! *(eyeing* CLAIRE*)* This is the Ibsen Festival, Miss Ford, not your daddy's Country Club pageant.
CLAIRE	Well, yeah.
ANTONY	You do realize it's only through your father's largess that you find yourself here at all. And speaking of "Endowments"... *(looking into house)* Claire's boobies are still far too prominent. Is there someone from frocks in front? You there, Rita, Wanda, whatever... Bind these! She's intended to look like a man, not some great pouffing funny uncle. Of course, Claire, darling, if you'd endeavour to summon up the least tidge of masculinity it would help!
CLAIRE	*(stunned)* 'Kay.
DIRK	You know, bro. About that trap deal...
ANTONY	Don't give it another thought, lovee. *(to* JULIA*)* You there, "Nora Knowitall," when Dirk descends I want

you to run 'round and close the trap with as little ado as possible.

JULIA   Me?

ANTONY   Understood?

JULIA   But that doesn't...

TRISH   *(clears her throat)* Ahemm.

JULIA   I'll try, but ...

ANTONY   You'll do more than try, my lady. Let's chunter through it once. Quickly!

JULIA   Excuse me, Antony. I wonder in that case if I might also move...

TRISH   *(coughing the word)* Julia.

JULIA   ...it's just that I can't see the trap from where I am and...

ANTONY   Hush! This isn't a play about Julia bloody Hudson!

JULIA   I realize that, but that move will upstage whatever...

ANTONY   No one gives a sodding sausage whether a snivelling peasant would or would not close a bleeding trap, but it must be done, you see.

JULIA   But Antony, I think I could accomplish what you want and...

ANTONY   *(crazed)* Utter hush! I expected more of you, Miss Hudson. Foolish of me, really. "She's not fresh out of drama school this time 'round."

JULIA   Antony, if you'll just hear me out, I think ...

[TRISH *moves into* JULIA'S *eye-line, and they exchange a glance.*]

ANTONY   Stop slithering about, all of you! S'like minding a bleeding basket of adders. *(back on Julia)* Now then, what seems to be the problem?

JULIA   No problem, Antony.

ANTONY   Supporting others beneath you, is that it?

JULIA   No, it's...

ANTONY   You see, I'm at a loss here, really. Assist me, won't you.

[CAROL, *a large, severe woman enters the auditorium. She moves quickly down the aisle to the stage.*]

JULIA   If you'll just let me finish...

ANTONY   You've very little to do in this one, except give focus to your fellow troupies, and you can't seem to manage even that without behaving like Betty Bloody Brain Dead. Now why is that, do you suppose?

[CAROL *has climbed the stairs to the stage. She holds a tray and is breathing hard.*]

ANTONY Stop snorting, Carol.

CAROL Sorry, Antony.

BEN Maybe I could help by…

JULIA Ben, don't!

ANTONY *(to* JULIA*)* You must realize we did go out on something of a limb, having you back at the Ibfest. "Difficult." A "difficult" actress, that is "the word" on you. "Difficult."

[JULIA *looks to* TRISH. ANTONY *sees this.*]

ANTONY What? Why do you look there? Do you require a prompt from "thingy" here to respond to a simple question?

[ANTONY *snaps his fingers.* CAROL *moves forward with tray.*]

JULIA No, Antony. I'm grateful to be back and…

ANTONY *(eyeing sandwich for the first time)* Crusts?!

CAROL Forgive me. *(humiliated,* CAROL *whips out a knife expertly and slices off the crusts)*

ANTONY *(to* CAROL*)* For a big girl, Carol, you've a very small memory. *(to Julia)* No, no it's simply that you *seemed* to be so clever, so motivated when you were with us previously. But now a "third peasant wench from the left" seems an impossible stretch for you. What's happened?

JULIA Nothing, Antony.

ANTONY Precisely! *(seizing the sandwich)* Stagnation, is it?

JULIA You seem happy with my work in the Greek and the Restoration.

ANTONY Don't confuse the issue. *(eating like a pig)* What's happened to you, eh?

JULIA I was just trying to help.

ANTONY No, no. You see I'm simply curious, Julia. Curious and rather disappointed. What has happened?

JULIA	Nothing.
ANTONY	Yes, I've heard as much. But I wasn't inquiring after your career.
JULIA	*(wounded)*
ANTONY	What has happened to you?
TRISH	Antony?
ANTONY	What's happened to Julia Hudson?
JULIA	*(losing it)* Nothing! Nothing! Nothing's happened to me!
ANTONY	*(success)* Well that's hardly my lookout!
TRISH	For God's sake, get off her back.
CAROL	Miss Lovell!
TRISH	She's just trying to motivate that shitty new move you gave her.
ANTONY	Oh, mea culpa, mea culpa. Mea maxi-sodding culpa! I'm so sorry, I have to be the great big meany who drags you all out of your primordial ooze and lifts you above this theatrical backwater, but I'll be buggered if I'll settle for anything less than world class! *(to JULIA)* I can tell you my lady, this sort of insubordination would never be tolerated at the National!
TRISH	If you're so goddamned unhappy, Tony, I'd really like to know what's kept you in this country for the last hundred years.
CAROL	Miss Lovell, we're lucky to have Mr Manley-Dunn!
ANTONY	*(without skipping a beat and with concern)* Oh dear. Patricia, under the eyes, great satchels, love, so puffy with the drink.
TRISH	You know I haven't had…
ANTONY	Couldn't you keep it down to a quart a night. At least till after the photos?
TRISH	*(stung)* You bastard.
ANTONY	*(weirdly berserk)* And Deidrie, Phoebie, Wandy, whatever…have someone dash off something for the neck… Patricia's neck. Conceal all that flaccid turkey flesh.
TRISH	Cheap shot.

ANTONY	And let's put her in a *real* corset, shall we.
TRISH	Don't push my buttons, baby.
JULIA	Antony!?
ANTONY	Something in cast iron, I'd imagine.
TRISH	Ya wanna go!? Ya wanna go at it!?
JULIA	Trish, Antony, please.
TRISH	While we're on the subject: What's happened to you?
JULIA	Trish.
TRISH	Seem's that's the question the press would like answered.
JULIA	This is my fault. I…
TRISH	What's become of Antony Manley-Dunn?
JULIA	Trish, don't…
TRISH	Did we catch last month's *Maclean's*?
ANTONY	How dare you!
TRISH	"Oslo's Ibsen Festival"…
ANTONY	Carol!
TRISH	…or Bored by the Fjord."
ANTONY	How bloody dare you!!
TRISH	No, no. I'm just curious and slightly disappointed.
JULIA	Trish, please.
TRISH	You used to be so clever, so motivated, so nearly human…
ANTONY	Sagging bitch!
TRISH	What's happened?
JULIA	Trish, stop! Antony, I'm sorry.
ANTONY	*(to* TRISH*)* How dare you!
JULIA	Antony!
ANTONY	How bloody dare you! Carol!
JULIA	Mr Manley-Dunn! Antony! *(having gotten his attention)* I'm sorry. Forgive me. This is all my doing. I…
ANTONY	I won't be spoken to…
JULIA	We're all tense.
ANTONY	…cheeky defiance!
JULIA	We just want to get it right for you.
ANTONY	I've given my life to you people…
JULIA	Of course. Of course you have.

ANTONY   Bloated Betty Ford reject…

JULIA   Antony, I'm sorry. I forgot my place.

ANTONY   Yes, well…

JULIA   It's been some time since I've worked under a *real* director.

ANTONY   I've half a mind …

JULIA   A master like yourself.

ANTONY   *(focussing on her for the first time)* What's that?

JULIA   A master…

CAROL   Genius.

SIMON   Visionary.

CAROL   You hear that, Antony?

JULIA   One can become so untrusting out there in the…

JULIA ⎰ Regionals.

ANTONY ⎱ Wasteland.

JULIA   Without any disciplined leadership.

ANTONY   Point taken.

JULIA   No *one man* to guide, to decide your every move, every thought.

ANTONY   Mmmm…yes…D'you know I've actually heard some so-called directors asking their actor's opinions. Imagine the chaos, the unbridled anarchy of actors thinking for themselves. "Trying things." What's more, I have myself, upon occasion, been approached with, "Mightent I *not* have an English accent?" In an *Ibsen*! Can you believe…I mean… No, no really. *Pas de jest.*
          [*Strange pause while everyone looks at* ANTONY, *who is lost in some demented inner dialogue.*]

TRISH   *(to* JULIA, *but looking at* ANTONY) Certifiable.
          [TRISH *and* JULIA *smile at each other as* CAROL *builds up the courage to say:*]

CAROL   Antony?

ANTONY   Um?

CAROL   May we move on?

ANTONY   No, Carol. We mayn't "move on," in point of fact.

CAROL   *(sensing a trap)* Why is that?

ANTONY   Because, Dumpy, I specifically requested a three-count fade up on that basket. That last attempt looked to be all of ten tedious seconds. *(suddenly upbeat)* And they say an elephant never forgets.

CAROL   Forgive me. *(touching him)* I've got a lot on my plate today and…

ANTONY   *(wincing from her touch)* Yes, well you don't leave a lot on your plate by the looks of you. Quickly then, sort it out while I deal with this trap nonsense. From Dirky's exit. Chop, chop!

CAROL   *(exiting to booth)* End of song, please.

[*Everyone scrambles.* BEN *exits the stage*]

DIRK   Hey, bro. *(pointing to costume)* What about my duds?

ANTONY   Just mark it, poppet. Go.

TRISH   *(singing)* You've stolen my heart and now I'll have yours. Like a pirate you'll plunder me here on the floor…

CLAIRE   *(singing)* You've stolen my heart and now I'll have yours. Like a pirate I'll plunder you here on the floor…

ANTONY   Dirky you're exiting. No. No, just mark it. Mark it, everyone. Yes, yes. Dirk's…gone. We're front of curtain. Now, Simon!

SIMON   Um…Yes…Ah. Ah? What's the line?

ANTONY   Concentration!

SIMON   *(acting)* Concentration! *(pause)* No, that's not right.

JULIA   "Enough!"

SIMON   What? Oh, yes. *(then, in character)* Enough! Enough! I say!

ANTONY   Now. Up, Julia! *(clapping his hands)* Run! For God's sake, don't dawdle!

SIMON   This is worse swill than is served at the inn.

[JULIA *rushes to the trap and begins to close it as:*]

CLAIRE   Maestro, I pray you, let us proceed.

SIMON   'Tis a dog's breakfast.

CLAIRE   How may I hope to improve, if I may not…

ANTONY   No! No! Useless! Useless bloody move. Have some common sense, girl! You're upstaging the entire scene. Must I think of everything?

JULIA   Perhaps if I was to move later…

ANTONY   Hush! I've the very spot. You'll move *later!* Just after the twins re-unite. Line! Someone! Please! Put me in the text.

JULIA   Giro's line: "Strange and unnatural."

ANTONY   *(grudgingly)* I suppose. You'll move to close the trap on...what is it?

DIRK   Strange and unnatural.

ANTONY   Precisely, poppet. Let's see it once. Quickly. Quickly!

BEN   *(to* JULIA*)* Anything I can do?

JULIA   Thanks.

> [*Everyone scuttles into position except for* SIMON, *who wanders about, lost.*]

SIMON   Is, is it the fight?

CLAIRE   *(unsure but, picking it up, as Beatrice)* Oh my brother...

SIMON   I'm lost.

CLAIRE   ...OrEEazo, found?

ANTONY   *(snapping fingers)* Or-a-ZEE-o.

CLAIRE   OrEEazo, found?

ANTONY   Useless.

CLAIRE   Can it be?!

ANTONY   Deaf actress.

SIMON   Beg pardon...

DIRK   Strange and un...

SIMON   ...but where are we? Am I...have we..is it the fight...or?

ANTONY   You're off!

SIMON   What's that?

TRISH   You're already off.

SIMON   Chased off? Oh yes, I see. We're *there*.

ANTONY   Get off!

SIMON   Sorry, Tony. I...

ANTONY   Bugger off! *(chases* SIMON *off)* Carol!

CAROL   *(v.o.)* The twins are re-uniting and...Miss Ford

CLAIRE   *(as Beatrice)* Oh my brother OrEEazo, found? Can it be?

ANTONY   Julia, what are you waiting for?!

> [JULIA *crosses upstage, reinventing the move and making it a lot less noticeable.*]

DIRK   *(as Giro)* Strange and unnatural.

BEN   *(as Orazio)* Beatrice! My lost sister and in this alien livery.

CLAIRE   Have I but slept and wake I now to find the sea has not claimed thee and you so grown to such a man.

TRISH   *(as Lucille)* Aye, such a man!

BEN   *(to* TRISH*)* Fair lady, how do you now?

TRISH   Spellbound as from some enchantment. I pray someone unfold this...
   [*The trap door is closed.*]

DIRK   *(cutting* TRISH *off)* Right. The churlish poet who this chaos penned...

DIRK {Blah, blah, blah
TRISH {Oh, for Christ's sake ...
BEN {Mr Hart, you jumped.

TRISH   Don't bother.

DIRK   Ace that...and then I truck over here... *(grandly removing his pirate disguise, sweeps centre stage for the epilogue)* and do the final bit.

ANTONY   The epilogue.

DIRK   Huh?

ANTONY   The final bit, yes. There, you see, no problem, when done efficiently. Now quickly, we've just time to run this once with technical bits and bobs before tea.
   [*Actors take their places. The trap door is reopened by* PATSY, *from below.* ANTONY *moves up the aisle*]

PATSY   Mr Manley-Dunn? *(as Puck)* Through the forest have I gone, but Athenian found I...

ANTONY {Carol!
PATSY {...none...

CAROL   *(v.o.)* Patsy, down! Set back. The twins are reuniting. Miss Ford.

CLAIRE   Oh my brother, OrEEazo, found? Can it be?

DIRK   Strange and unnatural.
   [JULIA *begins her move to close the trap*]

BEN   Beatrice, my...

DIRK   *(cutting him off)* The churlish poet who this chaos...

CLAIRE {Dirk honey, ya jumped.!
DIRK {...penned

ANTONY   Don't stop!

BEN   { But Mr Hart's skipped …

DIRK { …is Fortune sure.

ANTONY   Press on!

DIRK   *(ploughing on)* …Now Fortune's made amends…!

JULIA   Stop!

ANTONY   How dare you.

DIRK   …by writing each an ending…

JULIA   Dirk, don't!

> [DIRK *makes directly for the open trap, oblivious.*]

DIRK   …that begins ……

> [JULIA *runs towards the trap.* DIRK *gets there before her
> and walks directly into the open hole. He stands
> suspended over the open chasm for a beat, as in a
> cartoon. All register expressions of shock.*]

DIRK   Um!?

> [DIRK *falls through the open trap. Blackout. Violent
> crashing sounds, screams, tumble and thump down a
> flight of stairs to an eventual bone-crunching thud.
> The sound of an ambulance siren.*]

Scene Two

[*Later that same evening at a performance of the Restoration play,* Virtue Slandered. *Our point of view has shifted and we are now "backstage." Ambulance siren cross-fades into the sound of a harpsichord. It establishes quickly then fades under but not out as, in the darkness, a television monitor fades up stage right.* SIMON, *in Restoration costume and makeup, appears on the monitor.*]

SIMON   (*as Sir Foppington Lushlace, on the monitor*) Egad, ladies. The town prattles of nothing else. I assure you 'tis not mere gossip neither, for I have it from sources unimpeachable. They do swear it involved the Countess Lady Laydown and her manservant, Old Blind Bob.

[*Small Ibfest audience laugh as lights fade up.* PATSY *is sitting, stage right, at the stage management console. The monitor is just above her head. We see the back of the Restoration set, which is mostly the "backstage" side of a large bay window, set some four feet off the floor. When actors "onstage" in* Virtue Slandered *move into this window they can be seen by the real audience. Besides this window we can see: exits to the dressing rooms, entrances to "on stage," a small closet door marked "Janitor's Closet" (stage right), a big set of double doors marked "Rehearsal Room" (stage left), and a large willow tree which can supposedly be seen through the bay window by the Ibfest audience.* BEN, *in period livery, holds his powdered wig in one hand and his script in the other. He paces nervously, trying to cram.*]

SIMON   (*continuing, on the monitor*) The thing arose, I'm told, whilst they took the waters at Epsom. And I'll be hanged if she didn't get more than a dose of the salts.

[*Bigger Ibfest audience laughter. As* JULIA *appears on the monitor,* BEN *forgets his urgency and moves to watch her.*]

JULIA *(appearing next to* SIMON *on monitor, as Lady Valentine)* If the truth be known on't, Mr Lushlace, I am not this morning in the visiting vein. Perhaps my cousin the Lady Lustford will see fit to entertain but, as for myself, I'm afraid I cannot.

[JULIA *(as Valentine) leaves the monitor and* SIMON *(as Lushlace) follows.* PATSY *swivels the monitor away from us. At that same moment, Lushlace and Valentine become visible in the bay window of the set.*]

SIMON But, poison me, Lady Valentine. Ain't I just this second arrived? You wouldn't turn me out without so much as a *quel que chose* and a kiss.

Good day to you, sir. *(disappears from window)*

Gad! A pox on it, madam...

[SPUD *and* BUD, *the stage crew, saunter on. They carry a period desk and chair. The desk has a candelabra on it. They set all this down and exit as:*]

SIMON *(continuing)*...I am vexed in the extreme. 'Ouns, my lady. Temperament!

[JULIA *exits from the Ibfest stage, and enters (to us) "backstage." She is emotionally distraught.*]

BEN *(moving to her)* Geeze, Jule. You're really flying out there tonight.

JULIA Thank you, Ben.

BEN *(taking her in)* Are you alright?

JULIA I'm fine. You?

BEN Little nervous. *(pause)* Scared spitless. I never dreamed I'd actually go on for Mr Hart.

JULIA Know all your lines?

BEN Oh sure, but...

JULIA Then you can only be an improvement.

[*Sound of carriage approaching.*]

JULIA *(kissing him on the cheek)* You'll be terrific.

BEN Thanks. Julia do you think you might want to...

TRISH *(appearing in the bay window, as Lady Lustford)* Ah, Lushlace, your hackney's below.

[JULIA *moves stage left in anticipation of her entrance.*]

BEN See you out there.

SIMON   *(now in window with Lustford)* Scorch me madam, I'm sure I colour with vexation! Good day!

> [BEN *crosses to the vanity and tries to read his script.* SIMON *sweeps off the "Ibfest stage" and enters "backstage," to us, as* JULIA *exits the "backstage" and enters onto the "Ibfest stage."*]

PATSY   *(coquettishly)* Dos't desire I should'st run lines with you, my Lord Belvoire?

BEN   Thanks, Patsy. I better concentrate on getting through my own part first.

PATSY   Antony'd be a fool not to let you play Belvoire for the rest of the season. And if he does, I figured maybe I could play your role.

BEN   Mr Handy?

PATSY   I already know all your lines. All I need'sa break! It's tough, though, 'cause Antony only sees me as a lowly apprentice.

> [*Sound of a carriage departing.* PATSY *neighs into the microphone.*]

PATSY   I just gotta act, Ben, or I'll bust!

> [TRISH *and* JULIA, *as Lustford and Valentine rush from "onstage" into the window and look down.*]

JULIA   Did'st ever set eyes upon such a weather-vain-brained flutter of lavender?!

BEN   'Scuse me, Patsy.

TRISH   A Frenchified essence bottle! *(they laugh)*

> [SIMON *has perched on the period chair near* BEN, *and whispers to him as:*]

JULIA   *(still at window)* Ah, your company is tonic, dear cousin, and I am in dire need of physic, for my father will not relent in this sick-making business of marriage.

BEN   *(to* SIMON*)* God, that's awful.

JULIA   He threatens daily to parcel me off to that modish coxcomb!

BEN   Did you go to the hospital?

JULIA   That prancing, long-winded, odious, powder puff...

BEN   Both arms and both legs?

JULIA   Monsieur Foppington Lushlace. *(moving into room and*

	so disappearing from our view)
SIMON	*And* the bridge of his nose, shattered. I don't imagine Dirk'll be pronouncing "Brawhhhdwhaaay" too clearly for some time.
BEN	So Mr Hart is completely out of the season?
SIMON	Out? *(laughing)* Oh yes. I'm 'fraid so.
PATSY	Quiet, you dandies and gallants.
SIMON	It seems Antony has cavalierly cancelled the Commedia previews and we go back into rehearsal Monday, with someone they *hope* to find tomorrow at the auditions.
PATSY	Auditions? For what?
BEN	Giro.
SIMON	Antony insists there's no one in the company *up* to the role. So I suppose Carol will be *up* all night ringing agents.
BEN	Gee, I hope they find someone good to play Giro.
SIMON	Not to mention Belvoire. *(moving to props table and finding his nasal spray)*
	[CLAIRE *enters from dressing room as* PATSY *rings a bell.* SIMON *watches* CLAIRE *with great interest.*]
JULIA	*(v.o. from "onstage")* Someone is without, Coz.
TRISH	*(v.o. from "onstage")* Mouthpiece!
CLAIRE	*(calling from "backstage")* Aye, mum? *(deposits her wad a gum on the prop table)*
TRISH	*(v.o.)* The door, you baggage.
SIMON	Bugger of a role, Belvoire. I played it here in '79.
	[CLAIRE *perks up her breasts as:*]
SIMON	*(still looking at* CLAIRE*)* Did you happen to feel it/see it?
BEN	What?
	[CLAIRE *enters "onstage."*]
SIMON	My "Belvoire"?
BEN	Simon, I was six.
TRISH	*(v.o.)* Who's at the door, girl?
CLAIRE	*(coming into bay window)* It's your man, Handy, mum, with a great packet of letters.
TRISH	*(v.o.)* Letters?

CLAIRE	*(still in window)* Yes, mum.
TRISH	*(coming to window)* Oh, constant Handy. Cousin? I pray you, permit him entrance.
BEN	*(watching* JULIA*)* Julia's transcendent tonight.
SIMON	Yes…
JULIA	This Handy holds my very reputation.
SIMON	A miracle, considering…
BEN	Dirk's accident, you mean?
SIMON	To say nothing of being given the sack.
BEN	What?!
SIMON	Oh dear.
BEN	What are you talking about?!
PATSY	Silence, yon fops!
SIMON	The boot, the axe…
BEN	No!
SIMON	This one tonight, the Greek tomorrow, and then it's "between engagements" for our Julia, I'm afraid.
BEN	*(very upset)* But why?
SIMON	Apparently Tony's taken the stance that Julia changed the blocking…
BEN	What?
SIMON	…and precipitated the mishap.
BEN	But that's not true!
PATSY	Shhhhhh.
CLAIRE	*(entering "backstage")* Lady Valentine will have thee up, Handy.
BEN	What?
CLAIRE	It's your turn, duffus.
BEN	Oh, Jesus!
	[BEN, *completely discombobulated by the news, begins to enter "onstage," realizes he doesn't have his letters, flies to the prop table, grabs them, plonks his wig on, and rushes "on" (off).* TRISH *has exited from "onstage" and joins* SIMON.]
SIMON	They're an odious clump for a Friday, don't you find?
TRISH	Mmmm?
SIMON	This audience.
TRISH	Oh God, Simon. How's she keeping it together out

there? I'd have to be Tanquereyd to the tits. Trust that bastard to fire her then make her finish the week.

SIMON   Tony didn't fire her.

TRISH   *(hopeful)* What?

SIMON   He had Carol do it.

TRISH   Typical. *(touching him)* My place after the show?

SIMON   Oh?

TRISH   I don't want to be alone tonight, Simon. I'll meet you at Gabbler's?

SIMON   Is that wise? *(mimes drinking)* I thought surely you'd be commiserating with Julia until the wee hours.

TRISH   She doesn't want a big deal.

SIMON   No, I expect not.

TRISH   What's she gonna do?

CLAIRE   *(coming into the bay window)* Mayn't I show Handy where to put it, your Ladyship?

SIMON   She have any propositions/prospects?

TRISH   Back to waitressing, I guess.

SIMON   *(watching* CLAIRE *in the window, not really listening)* Mmmmmmmm.

TRISH   Wait a minute, didn't Ben mention he had an uncle who makes films? Maybe there's something there.

SIMON   Mmmmmmm, lovely.

TRISH   I think it's a real Mickey Mouse operation, but...

SIMON   Mickey Mouse?

TRISH   Industrial training videos, or something. But it's a place to start.

JULIA   *(v.o., calling)* Lady Lustford! Ho, coz!

TRISH   Meet you at Gabbler's, then.

[TRISH *sweeps back "onstage" as* SIMON *rushes to the props table and blasts some breath freshener into his mouth. He positions himself somewhere in* CLAIRE'S *exit path as:*]

JULIA   *(v.o.)* I have this second learned a thing from Mr Handy will make your ears burn.

TRISH   *(v.o.)* Leave us, Mouthpiece. I'll be bound, she has the most tattling tongue in all of Christendom.

[CLAIRE *exits from "onstage" and passes near* SIMON,

picking up her wad of gum from the props table.]

SIMON   Difficult crowd.

CLAIRE   Fffffff. I dunno. I'm like all in knots an' stuff from the stress round here, an' that. *(she rolls her neck then arches her back, thrusts out her chest)*

[*A huge blast of laughter from the Ibfest audience.*]

SIMON   *(watching* CLAIRE*)* Ah! They seem to be perky up.

CLAIRE   Hope so. *(she bends over, dropping down through her spine)*

SIMON   I rang you, over the break, but only got your cervix…

CLAIRE   Well, I just called my machine an'… *(she lifts a leg up to the side of her head)*

SIMON   No, I didn't leave a message…I thought it best I speak to you in pussy. Person! I thought you might be going dow/*feeling* down and uptit/set. Needing a soldier to cry on. You must admit it's been a day.

CLAIRE   I bin a couch case…like bawlin' my eyes out all afternoon.

SIMON   Yes, I know. Julia let go, Dirk mangled. It is tragic, my darling.

CLAIRE   No! I mean not going to Broadway. Ya get it?

PATSY   Shhhhhhh.

CLAIRE   Daddy says without Dirk the show's not going ta …

SIMON   Shhhhhh, darling.

CLAIRE   Like this was sappose ta be my steppin' stone, an' that. 'Cause a Dirk and his movie connections. Now it's toast! An' I'm trapped here in the salt mines doing eight shows a week like one of them little pets in one of them little wheels. *(beginning to cry)* An' fer what!?

[CLAIRE *moves to* SIMON *and throws herself into his arms, sobbing.*]

SIMON   Ohhhhh, that's it, darling. Let it out. *(he kisses her)*

CLAIRE   Simon! Aren't you and Trish…?

SIMON   What? No! Never. Friends! *Des amies, seulement.* Oh, God! *(kisses her passionately)*

[*A burst of Ibfest audience laughter.* BEN *rushes offstage.*]

BEN   *(slightly hysterical)* Simon!

SIMON	*(springing away from* CLAIRE*)* Ben, my boy. How you hiding up?
BEN	This is awful!
SIMON	Not how it looks, I assure you.
BEN	We can't let Julia be fired like that.
SIMON	Oh, I see.
BEN	What is she going to do?
CLAIRE	What am *I* gonna do?
BEN	We'll have to confront Antony as a group and… and *reason* with him.
SIMON	Ha ha ha.
BEN	Tonight, if possible. Get him to change his mind.
TRISH	*(v.o., calling from "onstage")* Mouthpiece!
CLAIRE	*(caught off guard, calling)* Yes mum!
TRISH	*(v.o.)* Some light, Mouthpiece! It's gotten as black in here as a critic's soul.
	[CLAIRE *dashes for the candelabra, grabs it, and enters "onstage."*]
BEN	We can't let this happen!
SIMON	Ben, Ben; Ben. It wouldn't be at all politic to be seen supporting Julia at the moment.
BEN	To be seen? By whom?
SIMON	Wake up, child! The flats have eyes. The walls have ears. Tony's spies and toadies are everywhere…
PATSY	Ben?
BEN	Well, I'm gonna do something!
PATSY	Ben, your costume change.
SIMON	Take heed m'boy.
PATSY	Ben!
SIMON	I mean, *no one* will employ her when this gets out.
	[*Sound of a carriage.*]
BEN	But she didn't do anything wrong!
PATSY	Ben! Costume change!
BEN	Oh, right. Sorry.
	[PATSY *and* BEN *exit quickly to dressing rooms as:*]
CLAIRE	*(at window)* Mr Lushlace has returned, mum. *(exits window)*
JULIA	*(v.o)* Lushlace! I'll not suffer that supercilious booby.

TRISH   *(v.o.)* We, coz, shall abscond by the back stairs and employ his carriage.

[SIMON *enters "onstage" by one door as* JULIA *and* TRISH *exit "backstage" to us by another. The women have made an "exit, laughing."* JULIA *immediately begins to sob.* TRISH *holds her.*]

SIMON   *(v.o.)* Lady Valentine, your servant!

[*A huge laugh and a round from the Ibfest audience.*]

TRISH   Honey…

JULIA   It's just not fair.

TRISH   I know. *(a comforting smile)* Something will come up.

JULIA   If I could just talk to Antony. Make him understand.

TRISH   Waste of breath.

JULIA   I have to do something. An hour ago I was telling myself, I could walk away from all this. But I set foot out there tonight and… *(pause)* I have to act, Trish. That's all I've ever wanted to do. Ever.

TRISH   There are other theatres.

JULIA   Two. That do the classics. And do you think I can get in the door? Not even an audition. It's Antony's done that, I'm sure of it now. Convinced everyone I'm difficult. No, Trish. I *have* to make him let me stay and then someway, somehow, prove myself.

[*Sound of carriage departing.*]

TRISH   Let me take you out after the show. I'm meeting Simon at…

JULIA   Maybe tomorrow.

[JULIA *moves to her entrance position as* CLAIRE *appears in the bay window.*]

CLAIRE   *(as Mouthpiece)* It appears you've been bamboozled, Mr Lushlace. For look there, the ladies make off in your coach.

SIMON   *(joining Mouthpiece in the window)* Well, dress me à la droit! This Valentine would try the patience of a stoic. Hail a hackney! I'll to the theatre, Mouthpiece, and fill the Lady Looselove's box.

[*Laughter and applause from the Ibfest audience. A "scene change" begins on the* Virtue Slandered *set.*]

Music up and we can see the lights change "onstage,"
through the bay window. SPUD *and* BUD *have re-*
entered "backstage," they pick up the vanity and chair
and enter "onstage" with them. SIMON *and* CLAIRE
have exited from "onstage" to "backstage." SIMON
grabs CLAIRE *and kisses her. She is taken off-guard*
and begins to pull away but, before she can, SIMON
gags and lets her go. He pulls CLAIRE*'s wad of gum*
from his mouth and hands it back to her.

SIMON   Darling, your gum.

[*As she takes it, he grabs her again.* TRISH *enters*
carrying a bonnet. SIMON, *realizing he's been caught,*
abandons his mauling of CLAIRE. CLAIRE *gratefully*
escapes to her dressing room. The lights and music
from "onstage" change again and JULIA *enters.*
"onstage."]

SIMON   *(moving to* TRISH*)* Not at all how it looks, darling.

TRISH   You bastard.

SIMON   The girl's uptit/sit/set. Shit! Upset. I simply felt she
needed a little…

TRISH   …diddling.

SIMON   Yes. No! Encouragement.

TRISH   Lying, lecherous old fart..

[TRISH *turns her back on* SIMON *and moves off.* SIMON
sneaks out in search of CLAIRE. BEN *enters, dressed as*
Belvoire. SPUD *and* BUD *re-enter "backstage" from*
"onstage" carrying a chaise, which they drop
"backstage" (just left of the willow tree). JULIA *moves*
into the bay window with the candelabra. BEN *moves*
close to the back of the bay window. They should be
extremely close but in different worlds. We watch BEN
watching JULIA. *There should be no question that he is*
smitten.]

JULIA   Oh la, my heart. *(sobs, then gathers herself together)* He
goes on… *(reading)* "and like a misdirected player
upon the stage, I own my performance contemptible,
but never its motive. For if any interest was considered
in this intrigue, it was yours alone, believing I needed

more than love to make me worthy of you."

BEN   *(whispering to himself)* "What is there more than love?"

JULIA   What is there more than love? Ah, look. It follows, here penned as if in very anticipation of my question. "Place and fortune." So, Monsieur Belvoire, you would cast me as the mercenary? *(moving from window)*

TRISH   *(moving behind* BEN*)* You look great, kiddo.

BEN   Thanks, Miss Lovell. You think there's any hope Antony'll change his mind?

TRISH   "Hope?" I don't know. I used to hope for a lot of things. Now I'm happy if my bladder makes it to intermission.

BEN   I can't believe...*(seeing* TRISH'S *tears)* Miss Lovell?

TRISH   It's the air conditioning.

BEN   Why is he doing this to Julia?

TRISH   They have a sick and complicated history, Ben.

BEN   Antony and Julia?

TRISH   Uh huh.

BEN   Wait a minute, you mean they were...? They weren't together...?

TRISH   She was fresh out of theatre school. Brief summer infatuation with her big deal director. It's hard to imagine now, but once upon a time *(with meaning)* Tony did have his charms.

BEN   But then she fell in love, right?

TRISH   Head over heels.

BEN   Her "ex" was in the company?

TRISH   Mmmm. I warned her never to get involved with an actor...

[CLAIRE *rushes on from dressing room,* SIMON *close behind. He is bothering her. He sees* TRISH *and stops.*]

TRISH   *(to* SIMON*)*...but what can you do?

[*Music, the lights dim "onstage." Applause.* TRISH, SIMON, *and* CLAIRE *rush "onstage."* JULIA *has exited "backstage" and collapses on the chaise.*]

SIMON   *(v.o., as Lushlace)* Madam, that creature of yours, that Miss Mouthpiece, has as much sense as a fly in winter. *(audience laughter.)*

CLAIRE   *(v.o., as Mouthpiece, bawling loudly)* Whaa!

TRISH   *(v.o., as Lady Lustford)* Silence, baggage!

           [BEN *watches* JULIA *for a second.*]

BEN   *(as Belvoire)* Lady Valentine, the image of your beauty portrayed abroad dulls i'th the presence of the original.

JULIA   *(as Lady Valentine)* Mr Belvoire, you flatter.

BEN   *(dropping character)* I don't, you know. *(pause)* I called you over the break but …

JULIA   *(getting up from the chaise)* Excuse me, Ben.

BEN   I just wondered if maybe you'd like to have dinner with me tonight, after…?

JULIA   That's sweet, but I don't feel up to it.

BEN   Sure. Okay. What about tomorrow? A date like. Anywhere you want to go.

JULIA   Ben…

BEN   Please, you can't just *leave*…without seeing me.

JULIA   Oh. *(pause)* Does everyone know?

BEN   I don't think so. Simon said…

JULIA   Simon. Everyone knows.

           [JULIA *collapses back down on the chaise and weeps.*]

BEM   Julia, Antony's crazy to fire you, you're the best actor I know.

JULIA   It's okay, Ben. You don't…

BEN   If I could be like anybody, I'd be like you.

JULIA   You'd be unemployed.

BEN   Julia, you inspire me. Every performance. Every rehearsal.

JULIA   You're sweet.

BEN   I'm not sweet. I'm serious. You're the reason I'm an actor in the first place. I never told you this before because you already think I'm too young… for you and so on. *(pause)* It was my first play ever. We came here with my school and I saw you perform. Carlotta Knudsen in *Grey Tide*. Our class came for the Ibsen that year. But I returned on my own and saw it again and everything else you were in. I had toyed with the idea of acting before, but seeing you perform, that was when I knew I had to do *this*. It was like a light turning on whenever you entered. More than anyone else on stage, you belonged. Remember when Carlotta was sentenced to death? I mean, I stopped breathing. You made me feel what it must be like to go through something like that. And it was all happening right at that moment, right in this room. You were living it. It's still here in my head. *(pause)* You know, I waited for you outside the stage door after that performance.

JULIA   You did?

BEN   You wouldn't remember me. I was even geekier then. I waited and waited and when you didn't come out and my bus was leaving I asked the guy at the stage door if he'd give you a note. And he said, "Well, that's her there. You can give it to her yourself." I hadn't recognized you. Carlotta seemed six-and-a-half feet tall and this woman was small and shy and… I realized you had performed some sort of magic and completely altered everything about you. *(pause)* Anyway, that was the day I decided I wanted to be an actor. An actor like you.

JULIA   Thank you.

BEN   *(pause)* What now?

JULIA   I wish I knew.

BEN   I have a suggestion.

JULIA   What's that?

BEN   Dinner tomorrow night.

[JULIA *considers him for a second, then smiles.*]

BEN   Is that a yes?

JULIA   *(coyly behind fan)* But prithee sir, what of my reputation?

BEN   'Tis secure in my keeping.

[BEN *looks deep into* JULIA*'s eyes. She lowers her fan and* BEN *leans in slowly to kiss her.*]

ANTONY   *(appearing from nowhere)* Benjamin, love, poppet… *(seeing* JULIA*)* Oh!

BEN   Mr Manley-Dunn.

ANTONY	*(ignoring* JULIA*)* You look smashing, angel. Came to wish you all the best with the understudy, *çe soir.* Are we up for a gentle late supper...?
BEN	I can't.
ANTONY	Tiddley pop! You're not going to put me off again, I hope? I believe I deserve a little diversion after the day I've had.
BEN	Antony, I have to say that...
JULIA	Ben...
BEN	... I think what's happened to Julia is completely unfair...
JULIA	*(pulling him aside)* ...this is between Antony and myself.
BEN	I know, but ...
JULIA	Please.
ANTONY	The boy has an entrance.
JULIA	I'll see you out there.
BEN	Excuse me.

[BEN *walks to his position and enters "onstage."*
ANTONY *begins to follow to watch his performance.*]

JULIA	Antony, could I speak with you?
ANTONY	We've nothing to discuss.
JULIA	I realize you're upset about losing Dirk, but you *know* it wasn't my fault.
ANTONY	*I know* nothing of the sort. Would you kindly move?
JULIA	Please, Antony. Be fair.
ANTONY	Ms Hudson, you forget your place.
JULIA	Don't fire me. I don't know why you're punishing me, but whatever I've done I don't deserve this banishment. If I seem difficult, if I ask too many questions, it's because I want to get things right.
ANTONY	For God's sake, don't grovel.
JULIA	I will if that's what it takes. I'm a good actress. Don't throw me away. Don't *dispose* of me like this.
ANTONY	This conversation is terminated.
JULIA	Why are you doing this?
ANTONY	*(calling to* PATSY, *who's not there)* Pesty...er ah Nipsy...
JULIA	Is it because I left here?

ANTONY	Where is that nauseating gnome?
JULIA	Is that it?
ANTONY	Will you desist?!
JULIA	That's all I can think, is that you're still somehow angry with me for leaving.
ANTONY	You flatter yourself. I put you out.
JULIA	That's not what happened.
ANTONY	Very well. Have it your way. In any event, I'm setting the ledger straight this time round, aren't I.
JULIA	Revenge? Is this all some sort of twisted revenge? For what? Because I left? Because I chose to get married?
ANTONY	Fat lot of good that did you.
JULIA	I was in love, Tony. I had to find out.
ANTONY	You've made your bed then…
JULIA	This is crazy. *(an idea growing)* You don't…You can't pretend we *meant* anything to each other…
ANTONY	Hush! I owe you no explanation.
JULIA	I think you do.
ANTONY	Very well. I don't like you! There.
JULIA	We don't have to like each other. Cast me in the shows you don't direct.
ANTONY	You are tedious, uppity, and, contrary to your inflated self-opinion, you've never been an actress of any merit. In fact, I've never believed a thing you've done.
JULIA	Then why did you hire me back?
ANTONY	Pity.
JULIA	*(crushed)* Let's say you're right. Maybe I've never had any talent. But you did, Tony, and you squandered it.
ANTONY	How dare you!
JULIA	There was a time you could illuminate these wonderful plays, but you've lost it.
ANTONY	Hush!
JULIA	You're a bully.
ANTONY	Utter hush.
JULIA	"Play! A strange word when he may make such toil of it!"
ANTONY	How's that?
JULIA	I keep tonguing that line like a sore tooth.

ANTONY   *(raising his hand)* I'll give you something to tongue.

JULIA   You make *play* impossible. Everything you put your hand to...

ANTONY   Bitch...*(his hands around her throat)*

JULIA   ...turns brittle and shallow

ANTONY   Brazen back-biting bitch!

[JULIA *stares him down. He drops his hands.*]

ANTONY   The fact remains that I am Artistic Director of this Festival and you are — what? Waitress?

JULIA   I'll act again.

ANTONY   I wouldn't stake my gratuities on it.

JULIA   We'll see.

ANTONY   Any hope you may presently entertain that you will ever again be cast in this country is a false one. I'll personally attend to it, I promise you. "Difficult, dangerous, and talent-free." It's a small community.

[*Ibfest audience applause and harpsichord music up as* ANTONY *exits.* JULIA *begins to have an anxiety attack. She becomes faint and collapses onto the chaise, fanning herself.*]

TRISH   *(v.o.)* Tell me, Belvoire, outright. Will you or no, assist me in this intrigue?

BEN   *(v.o.)* 'Tis impossible whimsy, madam, that you should be taken for a man, in any light.

[JULIA *looks up as if stung. Music begins.* SPUD *and* BUD *enter and force her from the chaise as they begin to cart it off. Some idea is growing in* JULIA. *During the following "onstage" dialogue, she moves downstage, left. When she looks up, she spots a grouping of styrofoam heads on a props table. One of them has a man's moustache, goatee, and wig on it. She considers it à la Yorick's skull.*]

TRISH   *(v.o. building to the curtain)* Tush! I tell you, Belvoire. I shall take on the form of a man. And in that guise reek revenge on my cad of a husband. I have in my time performed upon the stage, sir, and of the characteristics possessed by a man there is not a one I cannot counterfeit. Send for your tailor, sir. For I vow

that I, Lady Lustford, shall by next light be reborn as
your cousin: Major Comeuppence of Coventry.
[*Ibfest applause. Blackout. Music up and full.*]

Scene Three
Part One.

[*Onstage, at a matinee of* The Raj. *A fun-filled
musical romp set in Colonial India: domed temples,
palms, a gazebo. A spotlight up on* LLOYD GARRICK *as
Colonel Clive . He is atop an elephant with his wife
Lucinda (played by* TRISH*). They sing in light operatic
voices, à la Gilbert and Sullivan.*]

GARRICK	It's ripping to be a white man and abroad;
	Downright bully to be dubbed a demigod.
	It's capital to be British in Bombay,
TRISH	Where I'll teach each native how to play croquet.
GARRICK	It's obvious they adore us,
	Like their white and sacred Taurus,
	For we're British, blonde, and just a bit blasé.

[*A male chorus, all in military uniform, joins in.
Lucinda, and Clive's Indian servant, Sadoom, played by*
SIMON, *look on.*]

CHORUS	Yes, it's got a kind of glamour
	To be thought of as a Rama,
	And especially since were just a bit blasé.
TRISH	Oh Calcutta doesn't cut it in the sun,
	Wi'such heat how was the Empire won?
	The food, the flies, the service so slipshod.
GARRICK	Stiff upper lip, for Country and for God.
	Yet I too query since we got near,
	Why the sun's so blasted hot here?
TRISH &	
GARRICK	For we're turning brown, just like these turbaned sods.
CHORUS	Yes, although we like a bronzing,
	This heat winds us like a watch spring.

Hence we might run mad and kill some
turbaned sods.

GARRICK
& CHORUS

So mount your steeds,
Crying Queen and Country.
Charge Sikh or Hindi,
It matters not.
My bugle heed
To the bazaar quickly,
Like the goddess Kali.
We're bloody hot.

[*A military-type dance begins.* TRISH *as Lucinda and*
SIMON *as Sadoom exit "onstage" to "backstage" via
the gazebo, as the company of* The Raj *exit stage left.*]

Part Two
Backstage at The Raj.
[*As music and dance number continue "onstage" in
voice over.* TRISH *is "backstage," waiting to re-enter.*
PATSY *sits on the stool at the stage management
console.*]

SIMON   (*entering from "onstage." To* PATSY) Mingy matinée
mob. (*mob mob mob — reverb from "onstage"*) I swear,
if one more of those old biddies unwraps another
sweetie… (*sweetie sweetie sweetie*)

PATSY   Shhhhhhhhhh.

SIMON   (*ignoring her*) I mean, the din of cellophane out there
is positively deafening.

PATSY   Your mic's on.
[SIMON *hasn't heard. He crosses to* TRISH]

SIMON   And can you believe… The air conditioning! On the
fritz in a heat wave? (*wave wave wave*) Darling?
(*pause*) Look. You can't spend the rest of the season
not… (TRISH *raises her finger to her lips in a "be quiet"
gesture*) Not speaking to me! (*me me me*)

PATSY   (*to* SIMON) Mic off! Mic off!

SIMON   Up yours! Up yours! (*yours yours*) How dare you?

	(dare dare) How dare she. *(she she)*
TRISH	*(reaching over and clicking off his mike)* Your mic's on.
SIMON	Blasted thing! Patricia, please. You must believe… *(becoming aware of her breath and body odour)* Ouf. Ouf. Gin, darling. Breath, pores. Ouf. I thought you were on the wagon.
TRISH	Didn't you hear that crash last night?
SIMON	What?
TRISH	That was me falling off.
SIMON	Oh, darling. Just because I didn't make it to Gabbler's? Tic-Tac? I rang all night. Why didn't you pick up?
TRISH	I did.
SIMON	Then why…Oh, I see.

[*A pause.* SIMON *is hurt.*]

TRISH	What do you care? I'm sure you had your hands full.
SIMON	I swear, I was alone the entire evening.
TRISH	Oh, Simon. I wish I could believe you.
SIMON	Patricia, darling. How many times must I tell you I was simply comforting the girl. She was extremely up…set. Upset.
TRISH	Oh, God. Couldn't we just call it a draw?
SIMON	Darling.

[TRISH *looks lovingly at him then touches his face.* SIMON *kisses her.*]

PASTY	Psssssssssst.
SIMON	Mmmmmm?
PATSY	You're on!
SIMON	Oh, Jesus!

[*They sweep back "onstage" through the back of the gazebo.* BEN *enters "backstage" half-dressed as a street beggar. He has a clipboard and pen.*]

PATSY	*(chipper)* Salam, Aboo Ben Palmer!
BEN	Patsy, would you sign this?
PATSY	Me? Sure, Ben. Golly, you look worse than Miss Lovell.
BEN	We closed Gabbler's last night. I don't know how she does it. I left her talking to that bag boy from the A&P.

[CLAIRE *enters, dressed as a street beggar, with a cobra in a basket.*]

BEN   I am so depressed.

CLAIRE   Well it's not everyday a stint on Broadway gets flushed down the toilet.

PATSY   *(referring to what she's just signed)* What is this?

BEN   *(pulling it away)* A petition.

CLAIRE   S'thrown a serious curve into my five-year plan, I can tell ya.

BEN   You know, Claire. A lot of actresses would give anything to have your roles.

CLAIRE   Yah. Well they can have them 'cause I want what Tori Spelling's got.

            [JULIA *enters, stage left. She is incognito and carries a large gym bag. Making sure she is not seen by anyone, she: listens at the rehearsal hall door while checking her watch; hides behind the costume rack; then inches the costume rack over to the Janitor's Closet. All this takes place during the following:*]

BEN   What about Borgstadd?

CLAIRE   *(non-plussed)* Huh?

BEN   Olga Borgstadd.

CLAIRE   Ffffff. She done any movies?

PATSY   Ms Borgstadd's the most famous director of Ibsen in the whole world.

CLAIRE   Sounds boring.

BEN   She's directing the season closer. Well, that's something to look forward to.

CLAIRE   You are such a Gilligan.

BEN   Here. *(handing clipboard to her)*

CLAIRE   What is this, what?

BEN   We're asking Mr Manley-Dunn to reconsider dismissing Julia.

CLAIRE   As if!

            [*Ibfest applause.*]

BEN   I'm serious.

CLAIRE   You are gonna be so fired!

BEN   Could I have that back?

[LLOYD GARRICK *enters from "onstage" and crosses to his dressing room.*]

GARRICK   Well, they ab-so-loute-ly detested *moi!*

PATSY   Ben, could I...?

BEN   Come on, Claire.

PATSY   Geeze! *(quickly into mic)* Stand by for the *Untouchable* number. Bud, stage left to raise the Ganges. Stand by, please.

[BEN *has not completed his change and rushes off to finish it. Music and dialogue fading up as we move "onstage."*]

Part Three

Onstage at The Raj

[*Gazebo revolves to "onstage" façade, revealing* TRISH *as Lucinda, seated on a setee.* SIMON, *as Sadoom, serving tea.*]

TRISH   Left handed or not, I say, this Caste system is beastly confusing.

SIMON   Not in actuality, Memsahib.

TRISH   Dash it all, Sadoom. Don't contradict your betters. Now, let's have this "untouchable" thing out in the open, once and for all.

SIMON   Oh, dear! Oh, dear!

TRISH   Tell me. How does this barbaric Caste system operate?

SIMON   A thousand pardons, but it is not barbaric. And if our great white leaders wish to understand Caste, you have only to look at your own system of class. *(music, singing)*

SIMON   Memsahib, for all your western wisdom,
          There are some things you don't know.

TRISH   Sadoom, you are proving wearisome.
          So I'll give you leave to go.

SIMON   Before I do, let me say this to you.
          Or far better, let me show.
          In India we have a plan
          That's served us here since time began,

Which may appear
A trifle queer
On your first observation.
We call it Caste; it oils the wheels,
And, if at first you strongly feel
Our local customs ungenteel,
Reserve your condemnation.
For I expect that you will find
That we are both of similar mind.
For you have class
And caste like class
Is preordained in humankind.
Is preordained in humankind.

[*A musical bridge for* CLAIRE *and* BEN'*s entrance. As the* CHORUS, *they sing:*]

CHORUS   For you have class
And caste like class
Is preordained in humankind.
Is preordained in humankind.

[BEN *begins to play a horn and the cobra rises from* CLAIRE'*s basket. Lights cross-fade as:*]

Part Four
Rehearsal Hall

[*Lights come up on the rehearsal hall, stage left.* ANTONY *sits behind a desk and* CAROL *stands behind him. "Auditioning Actor #1,* KALOTCHKI,*" is in the middle of his piece.*]

ANTONY   Stop! Wrong! Bad! Horrid! Horrid audition! You call that an upper class English accent?! That wasn't English, that was an accent from the country of Hopeless! *(checking resume)* Where are you from? Kalotchki? Kalotchki?

KALOTCHKI   I'm a Canadian, sir. I was born here.

ANTONY   Well, I seriously recommend you change your surname, unless of course you wish to *forever* evade being cast in the classics. Dismissed!!

[KALOTCHKI *leaves. We have never seen his face.*]

ANTONY   This is what you call talent?

CAROL   Forgive me, Tony. It's the best I could do on such short notice.

ANTONY   Did you actually think I'd entertain the thought of ever using any of these cretins. Even as a *temporary* stop gap! And why is it so blasted hot?

CAROL   We're having a heat wave.

ANTONY   I'm positively suffocating! I don't know how you're still breathing under all that extra flab. Have all the windows been hermetically sealed?

CAROL   No, I've managed to pry them open this time.

ANTONY   That accounts for the flies then, doesn't it.

CAROL   Shall I close...

ANTONY   Just shut-up and fan me! Next.

[*Music up abruptly.* CHORUS *in voice over.*]

CHORUS &
SIMON   For you have class
                And class like caste
                Is preordained in humankind.
                Is preordained in humankind.

Part Five

Janitor's Closet.

[*As* CHORUS *sings, the lights come up on the "Janitor's Closet," stage right.* JULIA *stands behind a makeshift makeup table. She has a plastic dye cap on her head, and is wearing a janitor's smock coat. She has brought: hair-dying paraphernalia, a cassette tape recorder, an alarm clock, an assortment of makeup, a wig form with beard and moustache, towels, a garment bag, a gym bag with pairs of socks in it, a thermos, a small mirror, etc.* JULIA *is holding a makeup book in one hand and a styrofoam head in the other.*]

SIMON   *(singing in voice over)*
                The British more than any race

SIMON

    Know what it means to "know your place."
    You're number one,
    The rest you shun
    As savage heathen monkeys.

[During the verse above, JULIA has put the book down, and placed the styrofoam head on a shelf. She takes off her smock and hangs it up. She now has on a flesh-coloured leotard and tights.]

SIMON   *(continuing)*

    So Caste should come as no surprise,
    Don't blush and flutter those blue eyes.
    For I can't stand and sympathize
    Since me you've caste as flunky.

[During the verse above, JULIA has grabbed socks from her gym bag and stuffed both of her shoulders with them. The alarm clock rings.]

JULIA   *(finds it. Reacts to the time)* I'll never make it. Oh, God. Oh, God!

[Puts alarm clock down.]

JULIA   I mean... *(East End London accent)* "bloody'ell." *(presses play on tape recorder, lower range)* "Bloody 'ell." *(lower)* "Bloody 'ell."

[From the recorder, we hear in a very proper BBC accent:]

WOMAN   Acquiring an Accent. Tape 32: London East End.

[Then a male voice begins coaching in a "London East End" accent. JULIA repeats the words and sentences after him. This section is very rhythmic and is supported by what seems to be the "Untouchable" dance break on the Ibfest stage.]

VOICE   Blister.

JULIA   *(picks up styrofoam head)* Blister. *(touches her lip)*

VOICE   Sister.

JULIA   *(replaces the head)* Sister. *(picks up the spirit gum)*

VOICE   Kipper.

JULIA   *(unscrews the lid from the spirit gum)* Kipper.

VOICE   Clapper.

JULIA   *(pulls the top off)* Clapper.

VOICE	Clever.
JULIA	*(applies the gum to her upper lip)* Very clever.
VOICE	Proper.
JULIA	*(tacky test)* Proper.
VOICE	The clever Clapper sisters blistered proper kippers.
JULIA	*(fans her lip with her hand)* The clever Clapper
VOICE	sisters… *(bends in to look in mirror, spills spirit gum,*
JULIA	*realizes spill, and whines)*
VOICE	Soccer.
JULIA	*(whines more)*
VOICE	Dapper.
JULIA	*(looking for something to wipe with)*
VOICE	Scrapper.
JULIA	*(grabs toilet paper roll)* Paper.
VOICE	Governor.
JULIA	*(begins to wipe up)* Governor. *(tries to shake off a piece of paper stuck to her hands)*
VOICE	Helena.
JULIA	*(sticky toilet paper is all over her hands)* Ugh…
VOICE	Commoner.
JULIA	*(one hand then the other.)* Ughhhhh!
VOICE	You're a dapper scrapper, Governor, exclaimed Helena to the commoner.
JULIA	You're a …scrapper… *(gets toilet paper off hands, manages to get some stuck to forehead)*
VOICE	Render.
JULIA	*(drinks coffee)* Render. *(looks at body profile in mirror)*
VOICE	Ender.
JULIA	*(looks at bum in mirror)* Perky ender.
VOICE	Gender.
JULIA	*(turns to mirror)* Gender? *(looks down at her crotch)*
VOICE	Bender.
JULIA	*(Puts coffee down)* Bender.
VOICE	Surrender.
JULIA	*(thinking)* Surrender.
VOICE	Pretender.
JULIA	*(grabs one pair of work socks, one pair of dress socks)* Pretender. *(turns front)*

VOICE   Member.

JULIA   *(considers each pair)* Member. *(chooses dress socks)*

VOICE   Bigger.

JULIA   Bigger? *(holds up work socks)*

VOICE   Better.

JULIA   *(looks at tape recorder)* Really?

VOICE   The clever Parliamentary member thought better...
        (JULIA *stuffs socks into her crotch area)* and rendered
        the vote bigger on gender.

        [JULIA *has her hands down her pants when the voice
        says:*]

VOICE   Cough.

        [JULIA *looks at the tape recorder as lights cross-fade
        out on "Janitor's Closet" and up on* SIMON *and*
        TRISH, *with* CLAIRE *and* BEN *as chorus.*]

Part Six
Onstage at The Raj

SIMON   *(singing)*
                Ohhhhhhhhh!
                I may rise from lower state,
                As Hindus we reincarnate.
                For unlike class
                From caste to caste
                We may advance and change our fate.
                We may advance and change our fate.

TRISH   But we have class
                And class not caste

ALL   Is destined sure to rule the waves.
                Is destined sure to rule the waves.

        [*Music up and big finish. Applause.* CLAIRE, BEN, *and*
        SIMON *all bow very low and back out.* SIMON *is already
        groping* CLAIRE. TRISH *remains "onstage" and begins:*]

TRISH   *(singing as* LUCINDA*)*
                To rule the waves. Ah, yes. But at what cost?
                In this alien, strange, uncivil distant land
        (we hear static)

> From mother England I am súrely lost… .

CLAIRE   *(v.o.)* Simon, stop it. I gotta change.

TRISH   'mongst savage heathen we must make our stand..

SIMON   *(v.o.)* Oh, God. Claire, I want you!

TRISH   Or else in shame, creep home again, sea-tossed..

CLAIRE   *(v.o.)* Simon!

SIMON   *(v.o.)* What? Oh bugger…

TRISH   *(singing as Lucinda)*

> Oh home in distant climes
> I crave your chalky cliffs.
> Oh isle of green sublime
> I dream in hieroglyphs.
>
> Of sailing back one day
> And finding you've not changed.
> Of docking in Ramsgate…

Part Seven

Backstage at The Raj

> [TRISH, *as Lucinda, continues singing but the scene shifts to "backstage"*]

TRISH   *(continuing, v.o.)*

> …And feeling unestranged
> That happy home-come day.
> Ho-oh-ho-oh-home-come day!

> [BEN *is near costume rack, changing from beggar into front half of sacred cow.* SIMON *stands close to him using various drugs and medications.* CLAIRE *is behind the costume rack, just out of sight for the moment.* PATSY *sits at the stage management console.*]

SIMON   *(over* TRISH*'s song)* Now that sea of blue rinse have all taken to fanning themselves with their programs. Monkey see, monkey bloody do!

BEN   Simon, I've drafted this…

SIMON   And the coughing out there… Talk about "barking up a lung!"

BEN	Would you mind...? *(offering petition)*
SIMON	I thought that one woman was about to launch her larynx onto the stage. Oh no! Have I taught you nothing? *(looking around furtively)* What could you be thinking? *(rips up petition)*
BEN	Simon, don't!
SIMON	After tonight, Julia Hudson will be Ibfest history, my boy. But you, you have a chance.
BEN	I don't think I want one if ...
SIMON	Oh, yes. Easy for you. Other fish to fry.
PATSY	*(into mic)* Stand by for the "Dream Ballet" please. *(BEN exits)*
CLAIRE	*(appearing from behind the costume rack)* Simon, would ya do me up?
SIMON	That boy is far too reckless. He'll soon find himself on the wrong side of Tony...
PATSY	*(into mic)* Spud to the fog machine...
SIMON	...and out of a job.
PATSY	*(into mic)* "Dream Ballet" please.
SIMON	But I suppose with his film connections...
CLAIRE	*(turning, suddenly alert)* Whaddya mean?
	[CLAIRE *has gotten into a bodice that has six arms. An Indian Goddess.*]
SIMON	Ben's uncle is...ah...something to do with...Mickey Mouse. Disney! I've such a headache.
CLAIRE	Ben's uncle's with Disney?
SIMON	Head of Disney, I believe Trish said. Yes. Head of Disney. Would you breast just there, darling.
CLAIRE	Head of Disney?
SIMON	Temples, darling. Good. Ah, that's spot.
CLAIRE	Head of Disney?
SIMON	Ouch. Claire! You're using your nails! Claire!
SIMON ⎰	OUUUUUUCH!
ANTONY ⎱	OOOOUUUUUTTT!!
	[*Lights down on "backstage" at* The Raj, *as:*]

Part Eight
Rehearsal Hall
  [*Lights up on the rehearsal hall, stage left. This scene occurs right on the heels of the scene above.*]

ANTONY Get out! You're a waste of skin!
  [*We see the back of Auditioning Actor #2.*]

ACTOR But sir…

ANTONY And burn your Equity card! Burn it!!

ACTOR Please…

ANTONY And if perchance you make the unforgivable mistake of auditioning for anyone ever again, *do* invest in some sweat shields! There's nothing more sick-making than staring into the seeping blotches of your steamy pits while you gesticulate like some crazed ninny. Now piss off!
  [*Auditioning Actor #2 leaves.*]

ANTONY You call that a "name?"

CAROL But Tony, he has a list of credits as long as my arm.

ANTONY Yes, exactly. Stubby!

CAROL Darling…

ANTONY This cattle-call is futile!

CAROL Don't despair…

ANTONY There's no one in this country can play… Hang on! That's it.

CAROL Mommy knew you'd think of someone…Who? Who is it, baby?
  [*Lights down.*]

Part Nine
Backstage at The Raj.
  [*Immediately following* CAROL*'s line.*]

CLAIRE *(calling)* Benjamin Palmer? Ben?

SIMON Claire have you seen my…?

CLAIRE Where'd tha cute-lil' Ben go?
  [CLAIRE *grabs the head of the Sacred Cow costume and runs off looking to give it to* BEN.]

PATSY   Stand by to enter. "Dream Ballet," please.

SIMON   My Fakir's not here. Patsy, you've forgotten my Fakir! She hasn't set my friggin' Fak... *(seeing it)* Oh. Yes, hide it why don't you. *(getting into the bed of nails)* Claire, darling, would you do me up. I did you. Claire?

[*As* SIMON *turns back,* TRISH, *who has exited from the stage, stands directly behind him.*]

SIMON   Lovely ballad darling!

[TRISH *grabs* SIMON'*s crotch and squeezes.*]

CLAIRE   *(as Goddess, singing on a high-pitched note)* EEEEEEEEEEEEEEEEEEE!

[LLOYD GARRICK, *as* CLIVE, *runs on, downstage. The Goddess and Sacred Cow follow.*]

GARRICK   *(singing)*
A cry awakes me from a fevered dream.
A nightmare battle where I lead the charge.
Ahead an ambush and it's I who scream,
   "We all are doomed and Death he is the Raj."

[*They all do a sweep across the stage, as* SIMON *and* TRISH *exit and the lights come up on* JULIA *in Janitor's Closet and* ANTONY *and* CAROL *in Rehearsal Hall.*]

JULIA   Who am I kidding?

CAROL   Tony?

ANTONY   *(coming back from some deep reverie)* Unnnn?

CAROL   Tell mommy ...

JULIA   ... this'll never work!

CAROL   Tell mommy who...

JULIA   What was I thinking?

CAROL   What are you thinking?

JULIA   I mean, look at me!

CAROL   *(snapping fingers)* Look at me darling...

ANTONY   Unnn! *(then)* Dumpy, ring the agent...

JULIA   I don't have a prayer.

ANTONY   It's our only hope.

CAROL   But who's agent, pumpkin?

JULIA   Maybe Tony was right after all...

ANTONY	Travel agent, Dumpy.
JULIA	"Difficult, dangerous, talent-free."
ANTONY	Next flight to Heathrow.
JULIA	God, it's just not fair!

[A loud gong sound as JULIA *throws in the towel.* ANTONY *stands and closes his file of resumes. Mysterious Indian-type music begins.* LLOYD GARRICK, *as Clive, re-enters.* SIMON, *as the Fakir, riding a bed of nails, makes an appearance in the gazebo.* CLAIRE, *as the Goddess, re-enters riding on the back of the Sacred Cow (*BEN*).]*

CLAIRE	*(as* GODDESS*)* EEEEEEEEEEEEEEEEEE!
GARRICK	Fever speaks malaria I fear
	Never fond of shadows they seem queer
	Mind is weak, wait for the break of day
	Where once again I'll be…
	British, blonde, and just a bit blasé.

[During this "Dream Ballet" section, JULIA, ANTONY, *and* CAROL *disappear. The verse is sung and Clive, Goddess, Sacred Cow, and Fakir, sweep off, leaving an empty "backstage" area. The door of the rehearsal hall opens and* ANTONY *emerges,* CAROL *helping him on with his coat.]*

ANTONY	Run the car 'round, Dumpy. I can just make the five o'clock flight. Ring Binky. Have him engage an audition space and line up his best boys. He knows what I like.

*[*JULIA *enters stage right, behind* CAROL. *She is very convincingly transformed into a young man,* JUSTIN FAIR.]*

JULIA	*(as* JUSTIN FAIR*)* I say, Mr Manley-Dunn. Smashing of you to see me at such short…
CAROL	No. No crashers.
JULIA	But I gather you're…
ANTONY	Are you hard of … *(looking up, a chord of music)* Hello.
JULIA	I gather you're in rather a bit of the old sticky.
ANTONY	*(to* CAROL*)* Leave us. *(smitten)* Yes, rather. And you are?

JULIA   Fair, sir. Justin Fair.

       [CHORUS, *in voice over, burst into song.*]

CHORUS   It's ripping to be a white man and abroad

       [JUSTIN *and* ANTONY *shake hands.* ANTONY *tosses a*
       sheaf of resumes into the air. As the lights fade to
       black and the curtain descends, the CHORUS
       continues:]

CHORUS   Downright bully to be dubbed a demigod.
       It's obvious they adore us,
       Like their white and sacred Taurus,
       For we're British, blonde, and just a bit blasé.
       For we're British, blonde, and just a bit blasé.

END OF ACT ONE

Act Two, Prologue

[*House lights begin to dim as solemn, dramatic music plays. It builds and climaxes as lights fade to black. We hear cool applause. Lights up on the front curtain. Two masked Greek soldiers enter and bow. A Greek chorus (masked):* JULIA, CLAIRE, *and a third actor enter quickly and bow.* SIMON *as Cretinon enters and bows. He is not masked but has a bandaged eye.* BEN, *as Deadus, in a teeny-tiny bloody toga, and* TRISH, *as Hermineyers, in robes with bloody front, enter, and bow. They are also without masks. The curtain call so far has been quickly paced. But now, as the music builds, the cast turn to the curtain and wait. Finally a hand emerges. A follow-spot hits* JEREMY ATKINS-AUSTIN, *the star of* Pantilous in Crete. *He enters slowly, drained by his performance. Theatrically, he clutches the curtain for the mere strength to stand and does a very grand bow. The entire company bows again.* CLAIRE *manages to let her mask slip, revealing her face. She makes this look accidental. Blackout. In the dark we hear:*]

CAROL   (*v.o. speaker*) A rather tepid show this evening, ladies and gentlemen. With, of course, the exception of Mr Atkins-Austin.

Scene One

[*Lights up. We are "backstage" after the performance of* Pantilous in Crete. *Appropriate props and set pieces.* JULIA *dashes in from the curtain call, removing her mask. She collects her gym bag from a waste paper basket stage left. She then runs towards the Janitor's Closet. All this during:*]

CAROL   *(cont'd v.o.)* Your next performance is *Frozen Wheat* on Monday evening. Please note: Antony asks you all to "hang about" as he'd like to introduce you to Mr Justin Fair, who will be stepping in for Mr Hart.

JULIA   *(sees that the Janitor's Closet door is blocked by a large Greek pillar)* Oh, no!

> [JULIA *attempts to push the pillar aside as* TRISH *and the two Greek soldiers enter from "onstage."* JULIA *hides.*]

TRISH   *(to the soldiers)* So listen, boys. You realize that was Julia's last show tonight. I'm taking her to Gabbler's. Why don't you join us. First round's on me.

JULIA   Oh dear!

> [*As* TRISH *and soldiers exit to dressing room,* JULIA *resumes moving the Greek pillar away from the closet door.* SIMON *and* ATKINS-AUSTIN *enter from "onstage."*]

SIMON   ...and then what do we see in the curtain call?! Backs! All these *backs*, scuttling up the aisle, pulling on their coats, fishing for their car keys. Just when they should be standing and thanking you with their applause!

> [*On* SIMON's *second "manners" (below) the Greek pillar that* JULIA *is moving teeters and falls, just missing* ATKINS-AUSTIN. JULIA *hides again.*]

SIMON   "Where are your *manners!*" I wanted to shout. "Where are your goddamned manners!" *(crash etc.)* What in blazes...?

CAROL   *(v.o.)* Mr Atkins-Austin?

ATKINS   Uneh?

SIMON   Shoddy! Dangerous!

> [ATKINS-AUSTIN *holds up a hand to silence* SIMON.]

CAROL   *(v.o.)*...your limo's at the stage door, sir.

ATKINS   *(grandly, deeply)* Ahhhhh.

> [ATKINS-AUSTIN *sweeps off, taking the light with him.*]

SIMON   *(calling after* ATKINS-AUSTIN*)* Goodnight sir. Wonderful day off. *Days* off.

> [SPUD *and* BUD *enter, pushing on the quick-change booth.*]

SIMON   *(to himself)* Old bastard bellows blindly through *one show* and then it's "limo to the city." Bombastic, toffee-nosed, walking glottal stop! *(exits)*

> [SPUD *walks into the Janitor's Closet to get a broom, as* JULIA *scoots into the quick-change booth with her gym bag. She pulls the curtain closed behind her.*]

CAROL   *(v.o.)* Mr Fair, if you've already found your way backstage, please wait for Mr Manley-Dunn in the green room. Thank you.

JULIA   Oh God!

> [PATSY *with laundry bag in tow enters from the dressing room as* BEN *enters from "onstage,"* CLAIRE *hurrying after him.*]

CLAIRE   I gotta pool at my place. Like we could skinny dip, an' that.

BEN   Sorry, Claire. I have other plans.

CLAIRE   It's a way hot night…

BEN   Claire, I have a date with Julia. *(exits)*

JULIA   *(suddenly remembering)* Oh no!

CLAIRE   You are such a Barney. *(exits after him)*

JULIA   Oh God. Oh God. Oh God. Oh dear. Oh no. Oh shit.

> [JULIA *whisks off her headpiece and Greek robes, dressed as* JUSTIN *(trousers, shirt, etc.). She pulls out* JUSTIN'*s jacket and shoes from the bottom of the bag.*]

JULIA   Oh what a tangled web we…

JULIA   { …wahhhhhhh!
PATSY   { Ahhhhhh!

> [PATSY *has pulled back the curtain of the booth.* JULIA, *thinking fast, grabs her Greek robe and holds it in front of* PATSY'*s face, obscuring her view.*]

JULIA   Shhhhh, Patsy. It's me.

PATSY   Golly, ya gave me a fright, Ms Hudson. S'no one usually back here. Laundry?

JULIA   No! Yes! Here.

> [JULIA *dumps the robe on* PATSY'*s head then wraps a towel over her short blonde hair as she dashes*

behind the changing screen.]

PATSY *(as Ghost)* Revenge! Hamlet, revenge your father's murther!

> [TRISH *has entered from her dressing room. She is in a robe and carries a mickey of gin in one hand and a cigarette in the other.*]

PATSY I'll miss ya, Ms Hudson.

JULIA *(whispering)* Thank you, Patsy.

> [JULIA *closes the quick-change booth curtain then finds a robe which she pulls on over her shirt and trousers.*]

PATSY Now who's gonna direct my "Short Persons in Shakespeare" workshop? 'Night, Ms Lovell. *(exits)*

CAROL *(v.o. speaker)* Mr Fair, proceed to the green room immediately.

TRISH *(whipping back curtain of quick-change booth)* So this is where you're hiding out.

JULIA *(peeking over screen)* I just needed some time to pull myself together.

TRISH Weren't planning to sneak off, were you?

JULIA Actually, Trish. Something's come up…

TRISH People want to say goodbye. I'm dragging you out for a drink! *(pause)* Could be all for the best.

JULIA What? *(to offer of a drink)* No thanks.

TRISH Leaving. Getting out of here alive. This place has always reminded me of some sick old version of *Brigadoon.* Some sinister "ye oldie" colony, lost in time, with its own set of rules, its own twisted logic. "Oslodoon." The whole warped clan of us "lifers," paralysed; trapped here forever cause we're scared shitless that for us there is no longer any outside world. Far too old and wrinkled and — what do those casting assholes call it — *(with a gesture)* "theatrical." Far too theatrical for the tube. And, frankly, too goddamned tired to even want to read for some new "play." Some travesty, wanked onto the page by some tongue-pierced, trendy nineteen-year-old flavour of the month. Two hundred dollars a week at some hole in the wall to play an aging, heroin addicted lesbian transsexual vampire who has to show her sagging tits and eat her own vomit in the second act…

JULIA   Trish!

TRISH   Sorry. *(Scottish accent)* Auch, I'll be warning ya lass, ya come here for one season and in the bat of an eye, it's twenty years later and you've lost your looks, your mind, your will to live. The real world has slipped away and left ya behind. Left ya… *(spooky)*…in Oslodoon.

> [CAROL *enters backstage, smelling smoke, throws open the curtain*]

JULIA   *(startled)* Ahhhhhhhhh!

TRISH   *(startled)* Ahhhhhhhhh!

CAROL   What sort of school-girl hi-jinx…?!

TRISH   Ah, Jesus.

CAROL   Smoking, Lovell?

TRISH   *(innocently, Scottish accent)* T'weren't me, Miss Brodie.

CAROL   I smell cigarettes.

TRISH   *(taking a puff)* Perhaps it's the crew. *(blowing it towards CAROL)*

CAROL   Very well, Lovell, you're on show report!

> [BEN *enters backstage.*]

CAROL   Hudson, I trust your cafeteria bill's paid up in full.

TRISH   *(ushering CAROL out)* Let's go powder that brown nose of yours. Give the girl a moment to compose herself. *(slides the curtain closed)*

> [JULIA, *alone, puts on her moustache quickly.* CAROL *picks up the prompt copy from the stage management console and exits right.* TRISH *has another drink as* BEN *crosses to the quick-change booth.*]

BEN   *(poking his head in)* Here you are!

> [JULIA *covers her moustache with kleenex.*]

BEN   You okay?

JULIA   Why? Oh. *(sniffing)* A little emotional.

BEN   No kidding. Take all the time you need.

JULIA   Ben…

BEN   I still have to shower and change and…well, tell

you what. I'll meet you back here in fifteen? Oh, we
have to meet the new guy. Half an hour! They'll
hold the table.

JULIA   Ben, listen ...

TRISH   *(to* JULIA*)* Jesus, that bitch's so tight-assed when she
farts only dogs can hear. *(to* BEN*)* Libation?

BEN   No thanks, Miss Lovell.
[TRISH *pinches his cheek.*]

TRISH   *(to* JULIA *about* BEN*)* Remember skin tone?

BEN   Excuse me.
[CLAIRE *enters "backstage" in a tiny bathrobe.*]

CLAIRE   Benjamin Palmer your shower's runnin' but nobody's
home an I'm like totally outta shampoo, an' that.

BEN   Claire, I'm in a hurry.

CLAIRE   'Tellin ya this Julia thing's totally dead end.

SIMON   *(calling from off)* Claire darling...?

CLAIRE   *(needing to hide)* Eeeeyou!
[CLAIRE *jumps into the booth.* BEN *exits to dressing
room.*]

SIMON   *(calling)* Claire! *(pulling back the curtain, but not
seeing* TRISH*)* ...Oh, hello, Julia. Ah, Claire. I was
wondering if I might talk to you in privates...ly
Privately...something concerning a small moment in
Act Two.
[TRISH *throws back the curtain.*]

TRISH   Would that be the *climax* Simon?

SIMON   I thought you weren't sleeping/slapping/speaking to
me.

TRISH   *(pushing past him)* I'm not.
[JULIA *begins writing a note on a piece of paper.*
CLAIRE *listens nervously till the coast is clear.* CAROL
*enters right, from "onstage," and crosses to the stage
management console.*]

SIMON   *(calling after her)* Patricia, you're beyond comprehension.

TRISH   No, Simon.

CAROL   *(at the stage management console, into mic)* Important
announcement, please.

TRISH   ...I'm beyond caring.

SIMON   You can't pretend...

TRISH   *(to* SIMON*)* Shut-up!

SIMON   It's all very well for you to have *your* escapades...

CAROL   All those involved...

TRISH   *(yelling)* You're always the first one to bugger off an...

CAROL   Please!

TRISH   Spineless two-timing bastard!

SIMON   *That* from Canada's leading mattress.

TRISH   What?!

SIMON   Don't hit me.

CAROL   All those involved in the Commedia...

TRISH   Come here!

CAROL   Miss Lovell!

TRISH   Ah, screw it! I've had it with all this goddamned George and Martha! *(she exits)*

CAROL   Ladies and gentlemen, Antony has called the entire Commedia cast for ten a.m. Monday.

JULIA   Claire, would you please give this to Trish. *(hands note)*

CLAIRE   *(put out)* Tsk! Ffffffff!

          [CLAIRE *exits the quick-change booth, looking nervously around for* SIMON. JULIA *frantically continues doing her makeup.*]

CAROL   That's ten a.m. to begin replacement rehearsals.

SIMON   *(grabbing her)* Claire, darling. Please.

CLAIRE   Simon... *(getting out of his clutches)*...don't be such a hormone.

SIMON   Claire, I...

CLAIRE   *(with an unmistakable finality)* Take a chill pill, okay? *(exits)*

SIMON   Claire?

CAROL   *(calling after her)* Ms Ford?

SIMON   *(before he exits)* Oh, Carol. You won't forget about *practice.*

CAROL   *(into mic)* Ms Ford to the stage management console, immediately. Also, Mr Webber-Douglas would like to remind all team members of the Fouggenborky Ball practice, Sunday.

CLAIRE   *(entering, to* CAROL*)* What?

SIMON   Two p.m.

CLAIRE   What?

CAROL   *(into mic)* Two p.m. *(to* CLAIRE*)* Now, Ms Ford. Why do you persist...

       [*The phone rings.*]

CAROL   Don't move.

       [CAROL *picks it up and listens as* SIMON *says:*]

SIMON   Remind them all to bring their koenbeorgs and blatschtoppers. *(indicating elbow pads and helmets)*

CAROL   *(into phone)* Yes. Of course, Tony. Right away. *(holds on to phone)*

CLAIRE   *(impatient)* I'm here, okay!

CAROL   *(Into mic)* Mr Fair? Mr Justin Fair, Mr Manley-Dunn is waiting in the green room.

SIMON   Fair. Doesn't ring a bell...

CAROL   *(ignores him, to* CLAIRE*)* Now Ms Ford ...

SIMON   Carol, could you, ah...just a wee reminder...

CAROL   *(heavy sigh, into mic)* Fouggenborky Ball people...

SIMON   Much obliged...

CAROL   ...please remember to bring your, ah, koenschtoppers and your, tsk, blattnoggs?

CLAIRE   Like, hello!

SIMON   Ha ha. Koen*beorgs* and blat*schtoppers.*

CLAIRE   I'm freezin here, 'kay.

SIMON   *(enunciating clearly)* Koen-*be-orgs*...

CAROL   Piss off, Simon! *(*SIMON *exits)* Now, Miss Ford. If you're still having trouble with your mask, tell Patsy and she'll...

CLAIRE   I did! It is like *so* unfixable.

CAROL   Ms Ford...

CLAIRE   Word!

CAROL   I find that hard to believe...

CLAIRE   It could happen! *(having a little tantrum)* Anyway I feel like a total hemmorid takin' my curtain call in that butt-ugly mask, an' that. I mean like, like, really. How's anybody gonna know it's *me* unless they get ta see my...*(seeing* JUSTIN*)* Hi!

[JULIA *as* JUSTIN *has completed her transformation and is sneaking out of the quick-change booth.*]

JUSTIN   *(taken by surprise, as* JULIA*)* Claire!

CLAIRE   *(moving in)* Hi, I'm Claire.

CAROL   Ah, Mr Fair.

JUSTIN   I'm dead lost! It's a bleedin' labyrinth back here.

CLAIRE   Do I know you?

JUSTIN   No.

CLAIRE   But, like, you know me?

JUSTIN   Um… *(saved)* From the play!

CAROL   Mr Fair was out front this evening.

JUSTIN   That's right.

CLAIRE   Barf! Like *not* my totally best show, an' that.

JUSTIN   Don't be daft!

CLAIRE   *(not understanding, but liking him)* …Okay.

CAROL   Claire Ford, Justin Fair.

CLAIRE   Hey. *(sizing him up)* Like, you're the new guy!

JUSTIN   Yes, you could say that.

CAROL   Enjoyed the performance, then?

JUSTIN   Beside myself.

CAROL   Tony will be so pleased. He's got a big old soft spot for the Greeks. This way, Mr Fair.

     [JULIA *breathes a huge sigh of relief, having negotiated this round of introductions. The telephone rings again and* CAROL *crosses to answer it.*]

CAROL   One second.

     [TRISH *enters and pokes her head into the quick-change booth.*]

CLAIRE   So, like, Jason. You look famill.

JUSTIN   How…How d'you mean?

CLAIRE   Ya done any movies? Should I'a heard'a ya, an' stuff?

JUSTIN   No, never done a picture. The stage.

CLAIRE   *(hugely disappointed)* Oh.

TRISH   *(exiting the booth)* Claire, have you seen Julia?

CLAIRE   No. Oh. *(handing* TRISH *the note)* She had a dumb date with Ben, an' that?

JUSTIN   I should be off…

CAROL   *(to* JUSTIN*)* Change of plans. You're to wait right here.

(back to phone)

TRISH   *(reading)* I think we've both been stood up.

CLAIRE   Ben an' that? Really? *(to* JUSTIN*)* Catch ya later. *(exits)*

CAROL   *(hanging up)* Mr Manley-Dunn will be right down. *(excited for him)* He's taking you to dinner!

JUSTIN   No! I mean, that's very kind of him but…

CAROL   *(displaying her huge ring of keys)* Must lock up. *(exits quickly)*

TRISH   So…you the new man?

JUSTIN   …Yes.

TRISH   Welcome to the Ibfest, kid. Or as I like ta call it, "Waco on the Lake." I'm Trish.

JUSTIN   Justin.

TRISH   Waiting for Tony?

JUSTIN   'Ats right.

TRISH   Fortification?

JUSTIN   *(declining)* I expect dinner's not a bad idea, really. Toss the play around. Get a jump on things.

TRISH   *(with meaning)* I'm sure he will.

[CAROL *re-enters.*]

SIMON   *(scuttling in after her)* Carol, love. Something must be done about that nightly chorus of bloody watch alarms. I counted *nineteen* of them in my final speech.

CAROL   Not now, Simon.

TRISH   *(to* JUSTIN*)* Look honey, this is going to seem a tad rude…

SIMON   And a cellular telephone!

JUSTIN   How d'you mean?

SIMON   A telephone!

TRISH   Just relax and go with it.

SIMON   I tell you, it happens again, I-I-I shall leap from the stage and throttle the swine!

[CAROL *exits.* TRISH *grabs* JUSTIN*'s hands and applies them to her derriere. She throws her arms around his neck and kisses him deeply.* SIMON *turns and sees the couple.*]

SIMON   Oh, excuse me, I…Patricia? So! *(in a jealous rage)* Cock in the act, red-handed!

[JUSTIN *and* TRISH *come up for air.*]

SIMON   You really are the kettle, Patricia. You really are!

JUSTIN   This may look compromising, old man, but I was merely congratulating Ms Lovell on her performance.

SIMON   To say nothing of her work on the stage.

TRISH   Don't bother with him, Justin.

SIMON   Ah, the new man!

TRISH   Shut up, Simon.

SIMON   I demand an explanation, sir.

TRISH   *(mocking him)* "Ahdemaahdahnexplanationsah." *(to* JUSTIN*)* You'd never guess Simon's from Guelph, would ya, Justin.

SIMON   Patricia, you-you-you swore you'd never… *(to* JUSTIN*)* In any event, I'm L.A.M.D.A. trained! And that doesn't explain what…

TRISH   It's simple, Simon. Mr Fair is my boy toy and has been for some time. Unfortunate you had to find out this way, but — there you have it. *(to* JUSTIN*)* Welcome aboard, baby. *(*TRISH *saunters off, leaving* SIMON *and* JUSTIN *stunned.)*

SIMON   *(bursting into tears)* Patricia! Oh, Patricia I…

ANTONY   *(entering grandly, to* JUSTIN*)* Angel!

SIMON   Goodnight, sir. Wonderful day off. *(exits sobbing)*

ANTONY   Sorry. Fires to put out, you see. Norway rang. Frozen twits! Well, I see you've all met. *(taking* JUSTIN*'s arm)* Now confess. Did our little stab at the Greek live up to expectation?

JUSTIN   Felt like I was part of it, really.

ANTONY   Ah, the glorious gifted Greeks! Behold the altar of Thespis *(indicating the stage)* where we lay our vulnerable bodies bare and bleeding upon that *(as they exit)* Dionysian slab we call the stage.

BEN   *(rushing in, in suit and tie, a bouquet of flowers)* She wouldn't stand me up! She wouldn't leave without saying… *(into the quick-change booth)* Jule? *(sees a note on the mirror and picks it up)* Damn.

[BEN *reads the letter as we hear* JULIA *in voice over*]

JULIA   *(v.o.)* Dear Ben.

BEN   Damn it! *(breaking down)*

JULIA   *(v.o.)* Forgive me. Have landed the role of a lifetime. Must begin immediately. Further details best kept under wraps.

[CLAIRE, *all dolled up, tiptoes in behind* BEN*'s chair.*]

JULIA   *(v.o.)* If all works out will make appearance at your opening. Don't worry, Ben. Soon all will become clear.

[CLAIRE *puts her hands over* BEN*'s eyes. Blackout*]

[*A spot up on* ANTONY, *in audience, leaning against the stage.*]

ANTONY   *(reciting)* "Blinded!! my mother ravished, Zeus, my brothers eaten by their father." Oh what further woe can you heap upon these blasted and bloody shoulders?!" The irony is, of course, that Zeus has already ordered the poor blighter buggered by the entire Spartan army. Of course, the play is never done over here. Philistines on my board won't allow it. *(in a Canadian twang)* "It's farrr too lahng." I do realize nine hours is a tidge prohibitous, but bung in a dinner break and dub it an "event."

Scene Two

[*One week later. Lights up revealing the set of the Commedia, as in Act One, scene one. The cast are in partial costume.* CAROL *and* SIMON *seem enthralled with* ANTONY*'s story.* CLAIRE *is doing subtle butt-lifting exercises.* BEN *is depressed.* TRISH *is nursing a hangover.*]

ANTONY   Of course, Lord Larry was staggering in the role! Revolutionary. Imagine, the classical *simplicity* of: Larry, the text, and one small, hard, stool. *(pause)* Oh no, I could smell it right off: Whole, whole new movement! Naturally the press dumped on him. But never mind — as in all great movements, right on his tail, *Dame Judith* produced thee *biggest* Hecuba! I

	mean it was enormous when it came out! We were all of us stunned by the colossal magnitude of the thing! Right round the Nash and onto the bridge; the queues. Huge splash. *Huge!* Eventually hit the West End. I mean she *ran* for years!
SIMON	Ran and ran.
ANTONY	It was, after all, Dame Judith who… *(seeing that* JUSTIN *has not been listening.)* Are you with us, Fair?
JUSTIN	We starting then?
ANTONY	Starting? We've been back from tea for…
CAROL	Eighty three minutes, seventeen seconds… *(behind* ANTONY, *imploring* JUSTIN*)*
JUSTIN	Yes. I realize that, but as you were telling another of your stories…
	[*Everyone gasps and freezes.*]
ANTONY	*(ice)* "Stories?"
JUSTIN	We've only a week. I should think every moment counts. And with such a complex comedy…
ANTONY	'Snot Chekhov, love! It's *Wop Clowns On Bloody Parade!*
JUSTIN	I don't agree.
CAROL	Mr Fair?!
JUSTIN	With all respect.
ANTONY	Well you'd best "not agree" somewhere else, hadn't you? On the dole, perhaps.
CAROL	*(begging)* Mr Fair, it's been a trying week for Mr Manley-Dunn. No more confrontations, please.
JUSTIN	Surely there's room for discussion?
ANTONY	Are you deaf?! You're on shaky ground, Fair. Sans star power, completely unproven. A *stopgap*, frankly. Brutal, but there we have it. "Pirate entrance"! Places, Carol, please!
SIMON	Where, where from?
ANTONY	"Where from," exactly! It's all rather confusing with *two* directors!
CAROL	Don't upset yourself again…
ANTONY	Complete waste of a week's work with *two* directors! But there you have it.

CAROL   Tony, darling …

ANTONY   Why do I bother? Why do I even show up, Dumpy? Every bit of blocking questioned! Every guaranteed laugh poo-poohed! Every gentle suggestion quashed by a mountain of defensive rhetoric. And now I mayn't even trot out the *greats*.

CAROL   No, no, no. Not true.

ANTONY   No respect!

CAROL   We love you, Tony. *(trying to get a chorus going with the rest of the cast)*

SIMON   Greatest admiration…

ANTONY   Carry on, Fair. I'll just keep my *thirty years of experience* to myself shall I?

JUSTIN   I'm sorry, but I don't understand how another story about Dame So-and-so has any…

ANTONY   Oh. Oh! Far be it from me *or* a British Dame to shed any light on your precious *process*. Obviously I'm not needed here. I should just leave. I'll just leave, shall I? Shall I leave? ShallIshallIshallI? Shall I just bleeding bloody evaporate?!

CAROL   Tony! Tony! There, there. Fatigue. Nerves, pumpkin. Sit, baby, sit.

ANTONY   Ugh! Good God!

CAROL   *(in his face)* Sh-sh-sh-sh-sh!

ANTONY   *(trying to push away)* Pooh, Dumpy!

CAROL   *(intimate with him)* What is it, baby?

ANTONY   You have thee worst breath of anything still living!

CAROL   Forgive me.

          [PATSY *enters from the wings with glass of water, etc.*]

CAROL   *(averting face)* Here, here. Drink this. Alright? Alright now, my gentle genius? Shall we call it a day?

ANTONY   Absolutely not.

          [CAROL *pulls* JUSTIN *aside.*]

SIMON   It's going wonderfully well, sir. *(begins to massage* ANTONY'*s shoulders)*

ANTONY   Mm. *(he stares ahead, trance like)*

CAROL   Mr Fair, how many times must I ask you not to contradict Mr Manley-Dunn in public.

JUSTIN	Carol, I'm simply trying to do my job…
CAROL	Yes, but our Tony is…well, he's extremely sensitive.
ANTONY	*(to* CAROL*)* Fatso?!
CAROL	Yes, Tony.
ANTONY	Let's bash through a curtain call.
CAROL	Tony would like to set a curtain call. Final positions, please.
SIMON	What is it? Am I…?
ANTONY	From the end of the epilogue.
CAROL	You're off, Simon. Stand by, everyone. Mr Fair? *(to audience, with great sincerity and warmth)*
JUSTIN	And if in some slight measure we have pleased you with our play, Then grant this humble player the more pleasure back to say: [ANTONY *snaps his fingers*…] To please you is our best reward. To play for you…
ANTONY	They'll already be in the pub if you drip along like that, Fair. They're lemmings, love. They must be *led* to applaud. And this epilogue is nothing more than a clap-trap, and must be performed so.
JUSTIN	Clap-trap?
ANTONY	Clap-trap! Clap-trap! *Technique used to procure a round of applause.* Totally infallible.
SIMON	*(from the wings)* Infallible.
ANTONY	Simply raise your voice gradually as the speech draws to an end and make an alarming outcry… *(demonstrating)* …on the last few lines! This convinces them that the former must have been something superb, because it was so seemingly monumental and unintelligible. Hence they all clap to be thought intelligent. Alright? Now try it.
JUSTIN	But, Tony…
CAROL	Mr Fair!
JUSTIN	I'm thanking the audience here. I can't very well bellow …
ANTONY	Rubbish! Defensive excuse!
CAROL	Try it, Mr Fair. Please.

ANTONY	Clarion call on those final lines. Now. *(pause)* Quickly!
JUSTIN	*(trying)* To please you is our best reward.
ANTONY	Build it!
JUSTIN	To play for you our bliss. For sans your presence here tonight. I can't possibly. It makes no sense.
ANTONY	It's perfection.
JUSTIN	It's a cheap trick.
ANTONY	That's right. What? How dare you…it's *what*?!
JUSTIN	*And* completely contrary to the playwright's intention.
ANTONY	Spoken with him recently, have you, Fair?
JUSTIN	If you look at what he's written, it's obvious that…
ANTONY	I beg to differ. It isn't obvious at all. It's irrelevant.
JUSTIN	How do you mean?
ANTONY	Irrelevant because, as of now, it's cut. Alright? Got that, Carol? The epilogue is no more. There. Satisfied? Now. The lights will fade somewhat *earlier* and…
JUSTIN	You can't cut an important speech like…
ANTONY	Hush!
JUSTIN	If you have any other reason but punishing me…
ANTONY	There's nothing to discuss.
JUSTIN	No…
ANTONY	Right then.
JUSTIN	…perhaps not.
ANTONY	Pick it up. Line!
JUSTIN	Please accept my immediate resignation.
ANTONY	That's not the line, Fair. Carol? Put us in the text.
JUSTIN	I quit.
ANTONY	You can't do that.
JUSTIN	Watch me.
ANTONY	But, but, we're, we're we're a week to opening.
JUSTIN	Forgive me, everyone …
ANTONY	That's better.
JUSTIN	I simply can't create, bullied like this.
	[JUSTIN *begins to leave.*]
ANTONY	Bullied?! Tiddley pop. I'll show you bullied.

JUSTIN	Excuse me.
ANTONY	Don't be daft, darling. There's a sweet chap. Actors don't quit!
JUSTIN	This one has.
ANTONY	What are you? Mad? Or what are you? You you you…hastypants. Stop! Carol, stop him! Halt! Desist! Carol, please. Areyouareyouare you having me on? You you you sending me up?
JUSTIN	I'm in dead earnest.
ANTONY	Oh oh oh hot head! I won't be threatened, you hear?!
JUSTIN	It's not a threat.
ANTONY	Oh oh oh then. Oh then. Get out!
CAROL	(to JUSTIN) What Tony means to say is…
ANTONY	I I I shan't be held ransom! Go!
CAROL	Tony, hush. He didn't mean "go." He meant…
ANTONY	(increasingly agitated) Not cricket, Fair. Can't desert ship. We've we've we've only a week. Less than. Six days. Thirty-six hours. No time for new recruits. No no no time to learn this naf lazzi. I'm I'm I'm up against it, aren't I? Proverbial wall. There's an angel. (pause) How dare you. How dare you! To your room! I've caned for less. (pause) No no no clever darling love. Lovee. Poppet! No, I I I …me. Mine. Me. Me director. You. You there. Me tell you! You do. You quit? We don't quit? We carry on. We're British, Fair. (pause) I'll ruin you! Get out! Be good. You bad. Pooh you, you…you. Dumpy! Don't just ooze there, ew ew ew do something. Perhaps I was rash or or or have a rash or or or would you you you have a rasher of of ofofvavavavaaaaaaaa …
CAROL	Mr Fair. I think what Mr Manley-Dunn is saying, in his own way, is that there may be some room here for negotiation.
JUSTIN	That's all I ask.
ANTONY	Oh oh oh really?
CAROL	Tony. Allow me.
JUSTIN	Discussion. Inclusion.

ANTONY	Mr big britches!
CAROL	Now is not the best time...
ANTONY	*(mocking* CAROL*)* "Nowisnopthemessenime"
JUSTIN	I cannot rehearse another minute without we settle a few things.
ANTONY	I'll settle you. You you you uppity...
CAROL	Tony!
ANTONY	Toffey toffey toffey-nose!
CAROL	Antony!
ANTONY	What?!
	[CAROL *socks* ANTONY *hard on the jaw.*]
ANTONY	*(pleasantly)* Oh, Dumpy.
	[*As* ANTONY *crumples to the floor,* CAROL *sweeps in behind him and lowers him into* a Pieta *position. She then consults her electronic schedule as if nothing out of the ordinary has happened.*]
CAROL	He's booked right up. Monday, first thing?
JUSTIN	That leaves you precious little time to replace me if...
CAROL	I hope you're prepared to give a little, Fair.
ANTONY	*(groggily)* What are you plotting there, Dumpy?
CAROL	Private time with Fair. *(reading)* Board meeting from seven to nine.
ANTONY	Bugger the board!
CAROL	Not tonight. Then he's to speak at the Wine Tasting. *(to* JUSTIN*)* Perhaps over a glass of vino?
JUSTIN	I'd rather keep things on a professional footing.
CAROL	Very well. You'll have to meet back here at twenty-three hundred hours.
JUSTIN	Fair enough.
CAROL	Thank you. *(checking watch. To* ANTONY*)* Four minutes remaining. Shall we break?
ANTONY	Nonsense. Bash through the curtain call as planned. Quickly!
CAROL	Positions, please, for curtain call.
SIMON	*(as everyone else scrambles into final positions)* Am I...? Where...? Have we...?
ANTONY	We'll have music. Lights fading. Blackout! All get off stage, three bars legato, a small rallentando and then

a demi-quaver and a two count, lights up, count
four…then you'll hear a brisk bleat on the krumm-
horn and Simon enter first. *(all look to* SIMON)
Alright, let's try that much. And GO!

> [*Music. Lights fade to black but a bit of a spot
> remains on* SIMON, *who is hopelessly lost. Blackout.*]

Scene Three

> [*In the blackout the music segues from Commedia
> Curtain Call music into a Cowardesque piano intro.
> Some set pieces from the Commedia have been subtly
> arranged to give the feel of a hotel balcony in France.
> On this balcony, in ascot and dressing gown, sits
> ANTONY at what seems to be a piano, but is really an
> ornate chaise. At this point a keyboard protrudes from
> its backboard. A deco lamp embraces him in a
> romantic pool of light.*]

ANTONY   *(singing)* Life's just a bowl of cherries, so I've plucked
me one or two.
Oh what the hell, the truth I'll tell, I've gobbled
quite a few.
Don't care a fig if they're small or big, nor does
their gender matter.
Unripe or spoiled, pristine or soiled, I'll take'em
like a satyr.
My maxim's plain: You've nothing gained by
limiting your penchant
For Jews or Goys, showgirls, playboys,
lawyers…even agents.
(spoken) I draw the line at critics.
(singing) Decidedly "bi," don't be dreary and
try
To straighten or unbend me.
Decidedly "bi," Oh Ganymede and I
Are far too dementedly, contentedly

Decidedly "bi"…

[*A door in the auditorium opens and* JUSTIN *enters.*
ANTONY *continues to play the piano.*]

ANTONY   Darling!

JUSTIN   Ah, Mr Manley-Dunn. It is you.

ANTONY   Justi, dear. Do come in. I adore a theatre when there's
            no one about. So infinitely mysterious and sensual.

JUSTIN   I won't keep you, I …

ANTONY   (*raising a hand to silence* JUSTIN) (*singing the last
            phrase with meaning*) Decidedly "bi"…

JUSTIN   Yes. Well … It's very late …

ANTONY   (*claps his hands*) Ivories!

            [*A mechanical whirring from within the chaise and
            the keyboard slides out of sight.*]

JUSTIN   Have you given it any further thought?

ANTONY   You're looking unbelievably fetching in this
            damned stage light.

JUSTIN   If you'll just hear me out, make your decision —
            then one way or the other, I'll be off home.

ANTONY   Gracious. I do hope we haven't put you up at that
            frowzy little villa on the high street.

JUSTIN   No. No, I'm at the Gynt Pier Inn.

ANTONY   Quite right. (*offering his hand, impatiently*) Hand,
            hand. Up. Up! (*Grabbing* JUSTIN*'s hand and pulling
            him up*)

            [*Caught off guard,* JUSTIN *finds himself on the stage
            next to* ANTONY.]

ANTONY   Are you engaged for this dance?

JUSTIN   (*springing away*) Mr Manley-Dunn, leave off…

ANTONY   (*clapping*) Fag!

JUSTIN   What?

ANTONY   (*clapping*) Fag!

            [*More mechanical whirring, and a silver cigarette box
            appears magically from the chaise, opens and proffers
            a cigarette.* ANTONY *snatches two.*]

JUSTIN   Now about the epilogue…

ANTONY   (*one hand over his own mouth, the other outstretched as
            if to cover* JUSTIN*'s. With urgency*) Oh, darling.

Bollocks! Bollocks, darling! *(covering his ears)* Don't let's keep on about that. *(grabs lighter, hands it to* JUSTIN*)* Be an angel.

JUSTIN But, you see, it's a question of balance — *(begins lighting both of* ANTONY's *cigarettes)*

ANTONY There's a pet.

JUSTIN — Giro has developed a relationship with the audience in the *prologue* — *(declining offer of cigarette)* Thank you, no — that begs a resolution...

ANTONY You might have said. *(stubbing a cigarette out)* They are imported.

JUSTIN I mean to have my say on this.

ANTONY *(impatient)* Yes, I can see you've got your nasty little feet dug in. *(melting)* But let's be civilized about this, shall we? *(claps)* Cocktail.

JUSTIN Not for me.

> [*A tiny trumpet-like blast as doors on the chaise fly open revealing a miniature bar.*]

ANTONY Too late.

> [*A tinkly tune plays under as, music-box-like, the machine pours, mixes, garnishes, and delivers a drink.* JUSTIN *is stunned.*]

JUSTIN What on earth...!

ANTONY She has a name. *(the drinks arrive)* Can you guess? *(*ANTONY *passes one to* JUSTIN *while taking his own)* Sophie. Sweet. Chin, chin! Sit. Sit, my boy. Sit! *(*ANTONY *sits quickly next to* JUSTIN*)* Now, then. Where were we?

JUSTIN The epilogue...

> [ANTONY *grabs* JUSTIN's *thigh.*]

JUSTIN *(standing abruptly and crossing away)* Stop that!

ANTONY *(crossing quickly to cut him off)* What is it, my little Peter Panic?

JUSTIN Goodnight, Mr Manley-Dunn! *(shoves cocktail at him)* Or rather, goodbye!

ANTONY See here. You're not going to flit off into the night before we resolve our little dilemma?

JUSTIN   I don't believe you've the slightest intention of seeing my end.

ANTONY   *(downing his drink)* Quite the reverse, darling. *(downing Justin's drink)*

JUSTIN   I tell you, I will not tolerate such behaviour!

ANTONY   *(realizing)* Oh! Oh, I see. You thought I ... You silly scatter-brained little fool. It's simply that you seemed overly tense and I merely wished to... to reach out in some small way and comfort you. I meant no... *(breaking down)* I'm crushed you'd think me such a brute... *(pause)* Oh, yes. Go. By all means leave us.

JUSTIN   *(pause)* Antony if...

ANTONY   Don't. Don't apologize. Unfurl your wings and fly, dear boy. We'll find someone to play the role. Hey ho. *(pause)* What is it, darling?

JUSTIN   If I did in fact misconstrue your ...

WALLY   *(voice over speakers)* Mr Dunn, if you're in the building, would you pick up line four.

ANTONY   { Bother!

WALLY   { Emergency, long distance on line four, please.

ANTONY   Do hang about. Clairmont three five seven five here. What's that? Norway? I'm afraid you'll have to speak up. You have a bugger of an accent, you see. Now, what's this about? Olga Borgstadd, yes. *(pause)* What!? But, but ... but she *can't!* She's signed a bloody binding contract, man. Rehearsals for the Ibsen begin in a fortnight. Well, just tell her to put it off until she's fulfilled her obligations this end. *(pause)* No. No! *(pause)* Yes I *do* know what a bleeding double bypass is. Don't get all toffey-nosed with me, you insignificant meatball! Yah, yah, bloody yah! Kindly inform Ms Olga Borgstadd that unless she has an immediate change of heart my solicitor will be contacting her solicitor faster than she can say Laplander. *(slams down the receiver)* Blast!

[ANTONY *begins pacing. He is agitated and preoccupied.*]

ANTONY   That's it then. I needs must direct that drippy old pot-boiler *myself.* Oh, I positively loath Henrik Ibsen! Rain, angst, snot, and women with difficult names on perpetual P.M.S.!

JUSTIN   Look here. This seems to have upset you terribly. Perhaps…

ANTONY   Now you see, Justin. You see the trials of an artistic director. Sabotaged by that Hudson bitch, then a week lost catering to *your* incessant demands and now this Borgstadd cow just up and dumps the late opener in my lap and there we are: Cope!

JUSTIN   Tony, I do apologize for seeming difficult. But if … if you're willing to reinstate the epilogue, I could stay on.

ANTONY   What? Oh yes. *(fondly)* You great pratt. I'll be big about it, shall I. I'll allow you your precious little epilogue.

JUSTIN   Thank you, Tony. And…and without the… the clap-trap…?

ANTONY   Why, you can do it on your pretty little head, if you please. Right then. Friends?

          [*Offers his hand.* JUSTIN *takes it.* ANTONY *pulls him into his chest and tries to kiss him.*]

JUSTIN   *(struggling)* Let go my hand!

ANTONY   Give and you shall receive, I promise you.

JUSTIN   Stop this!

ANTONY   I can do wonders for your career over here.

JUSTIN   You're drunk!

ANTONY   I can make you, Justin. Oh, please. Let me make you.

          [ANTONY *pounces and a chase ensues during:*]

JUSTIN   If you hired me, sir, on the basis of some absurd notion of sexual favours, you *are* quite mistaken. By all means, find another actor!

ANTONY   Go ahead, work up a sweat. I like that in a man.

          [JUSTIN *is backed towards Sophie and falls into her.*]

ANTONY   *(clapping)* Places!

          [*Sophie jolts into action. A motor whirrs as restraining bands fly out of nowhere, intended to bind both of his arms. But because of the way* JUSTIN *has landed, one of his arms remains free.* JUSTIN *begins trying to tug himself loose.*]

(claps) Lights! *(the deco lamp swivels and shines a bright spot into Justin's face)*

JUSTIN   You can't expect to get away with this!

ANTONY   Don't budge an inch. You've found your light, you see. The house has dimmed. There's an air of anticipation. Cue the curtain.

JUSTIN   Curtain?! What are you talking about... Curtain?!
          (slaps his face while saying "curtain" and the restraining bands disappear) (JUSTIN *and* ANTONY *do a take)*

ANTONY   Clever chap! *(he claps)* Places!
          [*The machine springs into action again. Restraining bands out.*]

JUSTIN   *(slaps his face)* Curtain!
          [*The machine stops. Bands disappear.*]

ANTONY   See here, I call the cues. *(claps)* Place ...
          [JUSTIN *jumps free.*]

ANTONY   Hold your position.

JUSTIN   Bugger off!
          [ANTONY *pounces and traps* JUSTIN.]

JUSTIN   *(a blood-curdling scream)*

ANTONY   Do give us a great wet kiss.
          [ANTONY *plants a sloppy kiss full on the lips.* JUSTIN *begins to struggle.*]

ANTONY   Now see here. Behave, my boy!
          [*They are in a clutch and* ANTONY *turns* JUSTIN *upstage. Suddenly,* ANTONY *reacts in horror.*]

ANTONY   Good God! Your chin's come away, man. How absolutely dreadful for you.

JUSTIN   *(breaking away from* ANTONY, *clutching his beard.)* I'm fine.

ANTONY   Ew, what is that? One of those implant thingies gone awry?

JUSTIN   *(inching away)* Yes.

ANTONY   Hang on. I've just had the queerest... The soft and somewhat effeminate demeanour. And the voice, I thought it familiar.

[JUSTIN *grabs a deco statuette from near the lamp.*]

ANTONY   By God! I've been had. You're her. Hudson! You're the bitch to blame for all this.

JULIA   *(dropping character of* JUSTIN*)* Antony, what happened to Dirk was an accident.

ANTONY   Exactly what I shall say when the police find your body.

[ANTONY *grabs her throat and begins strangling.*
JULIA *hits* ANTONY *on the head. He falls over Sophie, landing just behind, his legs sticking out.* JULIA *lifts the statuette high to strike him again.*]

ANTONY   No, please. Don't let me die behind the sofa! It's so dreadfully *weekly rep!*

[JULIA *clobbers him a number of times, then collapses on the sofa, sobbing. (pause)*]

ANTONY   *(from behind sofa. Claps)* Places!

[*The sofa springs to attention and binds her in it.*
ANTONY *rises, bleeding a little.*]

ANTONY   *(thinking a moment)* I was rehearsing late, officer. *(taking a brightly coloured banner from the pole and preparing to strangle her)*

JULIA   Antony. For the love of God! *(trying to clap her feet)* Open! Um. No. Bravo! No, um?

ANTONY   Experimenting with some new moves, when I heard something.

JULIA   Places! ah... Stage! Oh God.

ANTONY   Will you cease! *(resuming theatrically)* There she was. A disgruntled cross-dressed thespian. Out of her mind because I'd terminated her contract. For just cause. For just cause! Just cause I felt like it.

JULIA   Curtain!

ANTONY   You have to clap, silly! You have to clap to activate our Sophie.

JULIA   Tony, be fair. I don't deserve this.

ANTONY   Fair? Is it fair, I've *wasted* my life in the colonies, teaching the natives the rudiments of the English stage. Fair?! I'll show you fair! She lunged at me, officer, hurling abuse and trying to ... *(getting idea)* *hang on...*to propel me down the open trap. *(opening the trap door)*

JULIA   Oh, please. Please.

ANTONY   Then a fatal misstep. An error in God's blocking and she fell. The banner terminally tangled about her throat. One single resounding snap and... *(he breaks down sobbing)* off she flew to Rep heaven. *(snapping out of it)* But first things first.

    [*He pulls the banner tight between his hands and moves in to strangle her.*]

JULIA   *(spotting the audience)* Oh, please! Please! If you believe in fairness, clap your hands. Clap your hands if you believe in fairness.

    [ANTONY *has an end of the long banner around her throat. When the audience claps,* JULIA *shouts*]

JULIA   Curtain!

    [*The bindings spring open.* JULIA *pushes* ANTONY *backwards over the open trap. Standing there, seemingly in mid-air, he looks down. He looks up. He smiles sheepishly.*]

ANTONY   I'll be buggered!

    [*He falls. Blackout. Screams and loud breaking and thumping noises. In the dark, the sound of a siren. This cross-fades into some banal 60s music. Kitchen sounds: eggs frying, clattering dishes, etc. Monitor fades up and we see and hear a woman sobbing quietly. She is in a housecoat and fixing breakfast.*]

Scene Four
Time Passing Montage

Part One
Backstage at Monday performance of Frozen Wheat.

TRISH *(on monitor as Sylvie, French-Canadian accent)* Brain dammage. Brain dammage. *C'est tres serious,* my son.

BEN *(on monitor)* I know that, Ma.

TRISH *(on monitor)* Pass me *ton* plate *la.* 'Ave you taught about da Four Hache or da Rotary?

CAROL *(v.o., on mic)* Lights Nine, go.

[*A light snaps up quickly. We see* BEN *(as Claude) hand on the light switch. He can be seen through the archway of a 60s-type kitchen-sink set. He stands in Claude's bedroom. There is a radio, and perhaps a bland wallpaper treatment, etc. Dressed in long johns, he grabs a flannel shirt and begins to put it on.* CAROL, *at the stage management console, swivels the television monitor away from the audience.*]

BEN Aw, ma. It's not the same.

TRISH *(calling to him from "onstage," then coming to the bedroom archway)* But dat 'ockey, c'est trop dangerous, my son. I don' tink I could take it, waiting up every night wit ton dinné in de hoven, 'oping it would be you walks true dat door an' not a call from da 'ospital …

["*Backstage" lights fade up during the above and we become aware of* CAROL *sitting at the stage management console. She is wiping her nose.* SIMON, *in a ski-doo suit, and* CLAIRE, *in a tarty 60s outfit with a winter overcoat, stand next to the console. An actor in a parka stands next to what can only be the exterior of the entrance to the house. He is shaking out his hands and rolling his neck and preparing himself for his entrance. This is* GARY WOLFE.]

TRISH *(cont'd)* A call to say, maybe, maybe, brain damage. *(leaves archway, sobbing again)*

SIMON   *(to* CAROL*)* Is he conscious, then?

CAROL   *(Into mic, holding up hand to silence* SIMON*)* Stand by, Sound *(heave and sob)* Five. *(to* SIMON*)* No, he hasn't come round. *(she breaks down completely)*

BEN   *(calling)* Ah ma...

SIMON   *(patting* CAROL*)* He'll rally.

BEN   ...just cause uncle Jim was hit by a puck doesn't mean the same'll happen to me.

SIMON   There, there. I'm sure Patsy will ring at any moment saying ...

TRISH   *(coming into the archway, switching off the radio)* Jimmyla ...

CAROL   *(into mic)* Sound Five, go. *(radio out)*

TRISH   ... he was never da same after dat, eh.

> [TRISH *looks at* CLAIRE *and* SIMON, *who are standing close together.* SIMON *moves away from* CLAIRE.]

TRISH   Bien. Look at 'im now. Not a taught in 'is 'ead. Selling dem newfangled ska-doos an takin on wit a girl 'alf 'is hage.

BEN   Louise.

TRISH   Louise, dat slut from da Rock.

CAROL   *(handing a card to* CLAIRE*)* For Tony. Keep it short.

CLAIRE   So, like — now what?

SIMON   Even if he revives, I don't suppose he'll be in any condition to carry on.

CLAIRE   So, like — the show's off, an' that?

CAROL   Tony wouldn't have it. Before blacking out he told Mr Fair he wanted us all to band together and take the Commedia on to opening. I must say, Fair's been an absolute pillar through all of this. *(to* CLAIRE*)* Composing a thesis, Miss Ford? *(to* CLAIRE, *pulling card back)* There are *two* M's in Bummer. Oh, Fudge!

> [CAROL *grabs wireless headset while speaking into console mike.*]

CAROL   *(quickly)* Stand by Sound Six. Sound Six, go.

> [CAROL *exits the stage management console. Howling wind is heard.* GARY *opens the door... He stamps the*

snow off his boots and begins coughing.]

TRISH   Mais 'ere come yer fadder now. Remember not a blessed word about yer sister gettin' 'erself knocked up by dat boy from da reserve. I'll tell to 'im myself after da curling.

[CAROL *re-enters, carrying a set of headlights. She has on a portable headset and mic to call the cues.*]

GARY   *(as Alphonse, entering)* Maudit she's as col' out dere as a nun's...

TRISH   *(off)* Bien, Alphonse. Not in front of da boy.

GARY   *(now off)* Colis. Dat Chevy. She won catch...

CAROL   **Stand by, Sound Seven and Eight. Lights Ten.**

BEN   *(entering his bedroom, grabbing his parka)* It's okay dad, Uncle Jimmy's picking me up on his ski-doo. *(exits)*

CAROL   **Sound Seven and Eight, go. Lights Ten, go. Stand by Sound Nine, Lights Eleven.**

[*Sound of ski-doo growing louder very quickly. Then a screeching sound.* CAROL *animates the ski-doo headlights across the set.*]

CLAIRE   *(loudly, Newfie accent, as Louise)* Now ya've done it, bye! Ya've put a great laong scratch on his Chevy. Yer brudder in lawh'll be pissed awf sumpin' fierce.

CAROL   **Sound Nine, go.**

[SIMON *opens the door. Sound of howling wind.* CAROL *mans the snow bag and begins shaking it.*]

SIMON   *(loudly, Newfie accent, as Jimmy)* Toss me da Screech der, Louise. I needs a bejesusbig slug behfore I face me prune of a half-sister.

CAROL   **Scene change, go.**

[SIMON *and* CLAIRE *enter "onstage."* SIMON *slams the door behind him as the lights fade to black.*]

Part Two *Hospital Room*

PATSY   ...and slamming doors and not talking to each other.
        [*Lights up on a hospital bed.* ANTONY *encased in
        plaster from head to toe. A small hole for a mouth.
        Some limbs are suspended in the air. It should all look
        complicated and painful.* PATSY *is sitting on the bed.*]

PATSY   Geeze, the fur was really flying. But with Trish and
        Simon, what's new, eh?

ANTONY *(muffled groaning)*

PATSY   Come again?

ANTONY *(a little louder)*

PATSY   *(not understanding)* Yeah, I guess. *(in a gush)* Anyway,
        I don't know if I told ya but I'm over my crush on
        Ben now. I had it bad, but I'm on the mend. Yep,
        things were pretty bleak there for a while but you
        know, the cast has really perked right up and I'd say
        it's all cause'a Justin. He's real cute. An' *good.* Real
        good.

ANTONY Eeeeee Ahhhhhh Aughe!

PATSY   Shucks. Can't make out a word with your jaw wired
        like that. *(imitating Antony)* Diction! Diction, eh? Ha
        ha ha. Aw, y'should just relax now, Mr Manley-
        Dunn. *(idea)* I know. I'll do another of my audition
        speeches for ya.

ANTONY EEEEEEEEEEEEE OOOOOOOOOOOH!

PATSY   Classical or contemporary?

ANTONY OOOOOOOOOOOH!

PATSY   Ophelia's mad speech?

ANTONY AUUUUUUUUUP!

PATSY   *(dramatically)* "God dild you! They say the owl was a
        baker's daughter. There's Fennel and rue for you, and
        here's some for me. We may call it herb of grace
        o'Sundays. Lilies for lunacy and columbines for..."
        [*Lights cross-fade from the hospital bed ... *]

Part Three

"Backstage" at a performance of Virtue Slandered
[...*to lights up on* BEN *dressed as Belvoire and* JUSTIN *in street clothes standing near the bay window.*]

BEN   Crazy! I mean totally nuts, I know. But she was so persistent. Wouldn't take no for an answer. Until she found out my uncle wasn't with Disney.

CLAIRE   *(as Lady Valentine, at bay window, in Restoration costume)* What is there more than love?

[CLAIRE, *with back to audience, waves privately to* JUSTIN *while she yanks a sheaf of script pages from her cleavage. She jams one page behind her fan.*]

CLAIRE   *(turning back to Ibfest audience, reading from behind the fan)* Ah look it follows, pinned/penned here as if in very anticipation of my question. "Place and Fortune." So Monsir Belvoire, would you cast me as the merceniny? *(exits out of sight)*

BEN   I wish you could have seen *Julia* play Valentine.

JUSTIN   *(pause)*

BEN   Boring you to tears? Julia this, Julia that. I just miss her. *(pause)* I miss her. Sorry. Look, I got a couple more minutes. You want to run your lines again?

JUSTIN   I should let you get into character.

BEN   No, I'm okay.

[JUSTIN *pulls out his script and hands it to* BEN.]

BEN   Um...from...Beatrice saying: "But fortune would not have it so."

[BEN *makes to leave,* JUSTIN *takes his arm and holds it.*]

JUSTIN   *(as Giro)* Hold, Orazio. *(pause)* Oh heart, take cover. Another dart hit home. The boy cupid launches the contents of his quiver. "Quiver," the word perfect, for all my senses do so now as I contemplate this lad ...

[BEN *and* JUSTIN, *as the characters, are looking deep into each others eyes. They hold the gaze, which soon becomes personal.*]

BEN   *(breaking it)* You have more to say ...

JUSTIN   Yes. Um...? Oh my, his cheek. That cheek as white

and twice as sweet as morning milk.

BEN   Justin, can I ask you something?

JUSTIN   Of course.

BEN   Have you ever been in love with someone who didn't love you back?

JUSTIN   I have, yes.

BEN   Break your heart?

JUSTIN   *(pause)* Oh, Ben. Just because your Julia's being cautious doesn't mean she doesn't care for you.

BEN   You think maybe she's just scared?

JUSTIN   Didn't you tell me she was married to an actor? Well. Once bitten, twice shy. I mean — if she's anything like me.

> [*They lock eyes. Smile. They become lost in each other.* JUSTIN *leans in and is about to kiss* BEN...]

BEN   I...I should probably ... um...I better...you know...go *(begins to leave, returns* JUSTIN'*s script)* ...act.

> [*Lights cross-fade down here and up on* PATSY]

Part Four *Hospital Room*

PATSY   *(in a Russian accent, wearing a babouska and holding a stuffed seagull)* I acted badly, I grew trivial, cheap.

ANTONY   *(groans)*

PATSY   Oh Konstantin, I didn't know what to do with my hands, how to stand on the stage, how to control my voice. You've no idea what it feels like, Konstantine Gavrilovich Treplyov, what it feels like to know that you're acting badly.

ANTONY   *(groans louder)*

PATSY   *(distractedly)* I'm a seagull. No, that's not it. Remember you shot a seagull? A peasant came along, saw it, and just for fun destroyed it. An idea for a short story. No, I don't mean that. *(rubs her forehead)* I'm a seagull. *(with a gesture)* Scene.

ANTONY   AUUUUUUUUU! AUUUUUUUUUU!

PATSY   Gosh, I'm getting hoarse. And that's just the first act.

What do you think of the title?

ANTONY   ERRRRRRRRRRSE! ERRRRRRRRRRRRRSE!

PATSY   It *is* a bit long. *"Everything Every Woman in Chekhov Ever Said."*

ANTONY   EEEEEEEET OUUUUUUT!

PATSY   Yah, I think it'd be a big draw at the small space. Or, or hey, you know, what about a Strinberg marathon. Listen to this...Oh dance...Oh death...

ANTONY   AHHHHHHHHHHH!

[*Cross-fade from hospital room to "backstage."*]

Part Five

Backstage at Performance of Pantilous in Crete.

[ANTONY*'s screaming cross-fades into* ATKINS-AUSTIN*'s howling on stage.*]

ATKINS   (*v.o. from "onstage"*) AHHHH! See Zeus!

[SIMON, *with horribly gouged eye, stands close to* TRISH. *She is holding her son's bloody head. They are awaiting an entrance, and call their lines to "onstage."*]

ATKINS   (*v.o. from "onstage"*) See your servant Pantilous, prostrate before you.

SIMON   Patricia?

CHORUS,
TRISH, &
SIMON   (*"onstage," all hissy*) Heeeeeed Zeusssss.

SIMON   I know I deserve the cold shoulder.

CHORUS,
TRISH,&
SIMON   (*"onstage," all hissy*) Heeeeeed his pleeeeeea.

SIMON   And worse. But...(*calling to "onstage"*) More grief is at your gate!

ATKINS   (*v.o. "onstage"*) Who dares interrupt my prayers?

SIMON   But for what it's worth... I've missed you.

CHORUS,
TRISH, &
SIMON   Cretinon.

SIMON   Terribly, really.
         [*all stomp once*]
CHORUS   (*v.o. from "onstage"*) He who slew the two-
         headed… (*all clap twice*) Theban serpent.
         [*all stomp once*]
SIMON   Forgive me?
ATKINS   (*calling*) Blind old Cretinon?
         [*all stomp twice*]
SIMON   (*calling to "onstage"*) Aye, lord. Son of the sorrowful
         union…
ALL   (*giving three sexual rhythmic grunts*) Uh, uh, uh.
         …of pitiful Pentax
         [*click their tongues thrice*]
ATKINS   (*v.o. from "onstage"*) …and the wanton Nippleous.
         [*All slap their bottoms thrice, then make a pop sound
         with their hands over their open mouths. CHORUS
         begins low moaning sounds.*]
TRISH   (*regarding him gently*) Oh, Simon…
SIMON   Yes, darling.
TRISH   I… Oh, your eye's come off.
SIMON   How's that?
TRISH   Your eye. Here.
         [*She hands him the bloody head, and begins to pat
         down his gouged-eye prosthetic.*]
TRISH   You're looking tired.
SIMON   Haven't slept much. (*he looks at her*) Patricia. I do
         apologize for … for being such an old fool. When you
         … when I thought you and Fair were … Hang on.
         (*to "onstage"*) The women hurl their limbs like javelins
         from the palace walls!
TRISH   Simon, do you think you could ever do anything else?
SIMON   (*considering this*) Well, I suppose I could pitch it a bit
         higher.
TRISH   No, I meant in life.
SIMON   Oh, I see. Why do you ask?
TRISH   Doesn't it ever strike you as a strange thing for an
         adult to be doing?
         [*All stomp twice, slap their bottoms twice, clap twice,*

and then pop their mouths.]

SIMON   Strange? How d'you mean?

TRISH   Oh, Simon.

[TRISH *moves in and kisses* SIMON.]

CHORUS   *(off)* A la lou gae!

SIMON   Darling…*(handing it back)*…your head.

TRISH &

SIMON   A LA LOU GAE!!!!

[*They exit, entering "onstage." Lights fade out here and up…*]

Part Six *Hospital Room*

[PATSY *is sitting on* ANTONY*'s chest with a guitar.*]

PATSY   *(singing the last line of a schmaltzy Broadway tune)*

ANTONY   AWWWWWWP!*(sobbing)*

PATSY   *(moved)* Gets ta ya, eh? Go with it, Tony. Just let it out. Justin says it's okay ta feel. Gawd, we're so lucky you cast him.

ANTONY   AUUUUUUUUUUUGH! *(moaning)*

PATSY   He's a dreamboat. Helpin' everyone. Well, the show's already a hundred times better. I mean, you can relax about that. Oh, get this! Since Ms Borgstadd's unavailable, the board's asked Justin to direct the late season opener.

ANTONY   *(violently)* OHHHER III EEEEED ODY!

PATSY   Yeah. Great, huh? Well, I better get going, but don't you worry yer l'il head. After tonight, I'll have twice the time to share with ya.

ANTONY   OOOOOOOO! OOOOOOOOO!

PATSY   You're welcome. So, anyway, happy opening, sir. Shame you won't be there but Carol said to tell ya to "relax 'cause we're in good hands with Fair."

ANTONY   ETTTTT EEEEEE OUUUUUUUUT!

PATSY   I know. He's brilliant in this show. It's gonna make him a star. And such a gentleman. *(checking around to see if they are alone)* Okay, I'm gonna tell you a secret. But you can't tell anyone. Cross your fingers.

Oh, it's okay.

ANTONY   UUUUUURRRRRRSSSSSSE!

PATSY   *(moving close to his ear)* I love Justin Fair. I just love him, Tone, and … and I think I'm gonna let him take my cherry.

ANTONY   UUUUUUUUT UUUUUUUP!

Scene Five
Backstage, opening night of the Commedia play, The Twins.

> [*Brilliant beams of stage light filter through the windows and doors and over the top of the set.* BEN, *in full costume and makeup, is pacing nervously. Unable to control his curiosity, he rushes to the monitor and watches. Another huge laugh from the house and a round of applause. He does a small victory dance.*]

CAROL   *(v.o.)* Patsy to the quick-change booth for Mr Fair's pirate change. Patsy?

> [BEN *looks around. He notices* PATSY*'s headset, dangling from the console.*]

CAROL   *(v.o.)* Patsy? On headset, immediately.

BEN   *(tinkering with the headset)* Carol? *(pause)* Ben, ma'am. Patsy's not here. No, ma'am. *(looking to booth)* I can't see her. Sorry, I've got an entrance.

> [BEN *moves to the wings and passes* JUSTIN, *who has just run in from the trap room.* JUSTIN *is removing his Giro costume as he crosses.*]

BEN   What a great house!

JUSTIN   Yes. Have you seen Patsy?

BEN   Carol's hunting her down. Sorry, I can't help you. I'm on. *(he exits quickly)*

JUSTIN   *(calling, dropping character, as* JULIA*)* Patsy? Damn. Oh gawd. Patsy?!

> [*Frantically,* JULIA *enters the quick-change booth and looks on the rack for the pirate costume. She pulls*

various costumes off the rack.]

CAROL   *(v.o.)* Patsy? Pick up! Don't make me come down there!

JULIA   *(sorting through costumes)* Pirate costume?...no. Pirate...no. Pirate...no. Patsy...no. Pirate ... *(pause)* Patsy!

[PATSY *is revealed bound and gagged with tights and pantyhose and hung on a hanger.*]

JULIA   *(pulling her down and laying her on the makeup table)* Patsy!

PATSY   *(groans and moves)*

JULIA   Oh, Patsy. Who did this to you?

[*Behind* JULIA, *a huge brimmed hat rises revealing* ANTONY*'s face. He is hideous: bruises, scabs, and plaster.*]

ANTONY   Eeeeeee eheeees. *(three guesses)*

[*Large burst of Ibfest audience laughter as* ANTONY *suddenly jerks forward.* JULIA *gasps and drops* PATSY*'s head with a thud.* ANTONY *has somehow pulled bits of costume over his body cast. If he is wearing tights they should be weirdly lumpy. Plaster and bandages should be sticking out everywhere. He has a wig over his bandaged head and some sort of jerkin. He moves in an odd, worrying manner, stopping often to push a bone back into alignment.*]

JULIA   Tony!

ANTONY   Ouuuu iiiiiiiiiii! *(you win)*

JULIA   Tony. Please, I'm on.

ANTONY   EEEEEEK AH EEEEEG! *(break a leg)*

JULIA   What?

CAROL   *(v.o.)* Stand by, Mr Fair, for your pirate entrance.

ANTONY   Ahhh eeeedddd EEEEEEK AH EEEEEEEG!

JULIA   I can't understand you...I...

[ANTONY *holds up an arm to silence her. She stares at him. Bunny in the headlights.* ANTONY *reaches up to the side of his mouth and grabs hold of a wire and begins to pull slowly. Teeth pop out onto the floor. Sound of flesh ripping and slushy glirping sounds as*

he pulls the restraining wire out of his jaw. Blood and
bits of flesh hang off it.]

ANTONY   *(gurgling)* I said: Break a leg.

SIMON   *(from "onstage")* Heard you the pirate's name?!

CAROL   *(v.o.)* Mr Fair, you're on!

[JULIA *bolts from the quick-change booth and runs to*
the console, snatching up the headset. ANTONY *hobbles*
after her.]

JULIA   Carol, help! Carol …

[ANTONY *rips the headset out of the console.*]

SIMON   *(from "onstage," loudly)* Heard you the pirate's name?
[*A huge laugh from Ibfest audience.*]

ANTONY   Slaying them out there. *(pulling a scalpel from his*
sling) What a coincidence.

JULIA   Antony, don't. Don't do this.

ANTONY   Merely some last minute cuts, darling. But they're
vital.

[ANTONY *raises the scalpel over his head and rushes at*
JULIA, *gurgling.* JULIA *ducks out of the way and runs*
towards the dressing rooms, ANTONY *in hot pursuit.*
CAROL *appears backstage, running.*]

Scene Six
Set revolves to reveal "onstage" at the opening night
performance of The Twins

[SIMON *and* CLAIRE *stand stage left.* TRISH *and* BEN
stage right. The painted curtain on the little stage
separates the two couples.]

SIMON   Heard you the pirate's name?
[*Everyone is frozen.* SIMON *is breathing hard, looking*
to TRISH *for help.*]
Ha ha ha. Ahhhh…perhaps I misunderstood? Ha ha
ha. Heard you the pirate's name? *(silence)* So …
(deciding to desert) Perhaps, I'll scat/scout abat. Make
certain there's none of those pirates. *(exits)*

TRISH   *(after a short stunned silence, improvising)* Orazio, I've had the strangest...*thing*... happen. A *vision*, in fact.

BEN   *(following suit)* A vision, sweet lady?

TRISH   Yes. You are a twin.

BEN   Yes, I know.

TRISH   And you seek your sister?

BEN   Aye, my lady.

TRISH   She yet lives!

BEN   May I hope?

TRISH   You may. She yet lives... *(cueing* CLAIRE*)* ...directly behind that curtain.

BEN   *(calling)* Beatrice?

CLAIRE   But...?

BEN   Beatrice?

CLAIRE   *(hesitant, then)* Could it be?

> [BEN *pulls back the curtain. They see each other.* BEN *and* CLAIRE *pick up the lines.*]

BEN   My nurse was grey and toothless.

CLAIRE   And mine. She sang: *(singing)* Sleep by the river..

BEN   Drowse by the shore...

BEN &
CLAIRE   Sail in the moon, child I adore. *(singing stops)*

CLAIRE   Oh my brother, Orazio, found. Can it be?

BEN   Beatrice! My lost sister and in this alien livery.

CLAIRE   Have I but slept and wake I now to find the sea has not claimed thee and you so grown to such a man.

TRISH   Aye, such a man!

BEN   *(crossing to* TRISH *with* CLAIRE *in tow)* Fair lady, how do you now?

TRISH   *(with meaning)* Spellbound as from some enchantment. *(pause)* Well. *(pause, improvising)* I've never been a religious woman. Orazio, Beatrice. But see, see how I prostrate myself here and beg the patron of all players to lead us from this turmoil. *(with meaning to the booth)* Oh, Saint Carol! Blessed Carol, you who organize and manage, hear my humble prayer. Give us a sign!

> [PATSY, *in improvised pirate's costume, comes sailing*

across the stage on a rope.]

PATSY Ahhhhhhhhhhhhhhhhhhhhhhhhhhhhhhhhhh!

[*She has overshot and exits the other side.*]

TRISH Holy shit!

PATSY *(running back in, improvising)* Aguzzio, the pirate, at your service. Ha ha! I'm here. I am the pirate and I'm here! *(looking about wildly)* Where is he? Where be the villain?

TRISH *(to BEN)* Orazio, fetch back the Maestro.

[BEN *extricates himself, then tries to figure out which way to exit logically.*]

PATSY *(fiercely)* Cowardly blighter! I'll nay rest till his debt be paid or his troat be slit and his scurvy carcass hangs from the yardarm. *(pulls CLAIRE's sword from her scabbard)* Where be that lily-livered cur?

[*Just as BEN gets to the exit, CAROL comes crashing out of the inn doors, in improvised pirate costume. She is still wearing a dress and carries the prompt book. She is breathing extremely hard.*]

TRISH Good God!

PATSY Naught ta fear. *(saving the moment)* This be ... me mate...Mean *(noticing CAROL's skirt)* ... Carol Aguzzio, fiercest pirate that ever sculled a midmast. And I'll be thinkin she's got a queer tale to tell. Spill yer guts, me beauty.

CAROL *(Looking to the script, confused)* ...um ...

PATSY *(to audience)* Still getting her landlegs.

TRISH *(dropping character)* Oh, Patsy...

PATSY Harrrr, Patsy's me nome de plume...

TRISH ... it's all gone to ratshit.

PATSY *(accusingly, in character)* Who blew the gaff!?

TRISH *(pause)* Ladies and gentlemen...

PATSY *(desperate to keep it going)* We can still brings her inta port. Carol, summon the Duke's men...an' get some'a them boys from Bedlam Island. *(to twins)* One of ya's haul in the Maestro. Now as I was tellin' ya... The law, Carol, dispatch! ... I've a queer tale ta tell.

SIMON	*(bursting through one of the flats)* Tony's come unhinged!
PATSY	Queer tale in a nutshell!
SIMON	Save yourselves!
	[SIMON *runs and hides behind the little-stage curtain.* ANTONY *enters.* SIMON *and* ANTONY *should now coincidentally be costumed somewhat alike.*]
ANTONY	Kill you kill, kill, I'll kill you!
ALL	Tony!? My God! Tony...
	[ANTONY *runs around madly searching for* JULIA. *He pushes people aside, upsets props etc.*]
ANTONY	Where are youyouyouuou shammer, show yourself, slyboots! You can't hide from me. *(throws back curtain, exposing* SIMON*)*
SIMON	'Didn't think it was going *that* badly, old boy...
ANTONY	Ahhhhhhhhhhh! Come out here, coward! *(grabbing* CLAIRE, *scalpel to her throat)*...Or it's another nose-job for the princess.
CLAIRE	As if. Ouch!
BEN	Tony.
SIMON	Tony old man...
BEN {	Tony!
TRISH	You're not yourself, Tony.
PATSY	*(speaking to audience)* And who *be* this Tony, you may well asks yourselves?
ANTONY	*(shrieking)* Utter hush!
JUSTIN	*(entering as an elegant pirate, gallantly from staircase of the inn)* Antonio de Spavento. Deranged evil twin of our gibbering Maestro! And true author of all our woe. Unhand the boy, villain.
ANTONY	It's a disguise! A ruse. You're not...
JUSTIN	Clever! Quite right, Antonio. I am no pirate. I stand before you: *(tossing off pirate disguise)* Giro Vesposi, proud player.
ANTONY	No!
JUSTIN	And I've come to reclaim our stage! *(swashing down stairs)*
PATSY	Hurrah!

ANTONY   *(casting* CLAIRE *aside)* Over my dead body!

JUSTIN   Who is with me!?

PATSY   I'll ships out with ya.

ANTONY   Keep your places!

BEN   I'm with you, sir.

ANTONY   Are all of you mad? She's...

JUSTIN   Throw down your weapon.

ANTONY   *(feeling trapped)* How dare you! How bloody dare you!

PATSY   Sail alongside and board him!

ANTONY   *(to the booth)* Carol! Carol!

> [ANTONY *turns and bolts from the stage, taking*
> CLAIRE *hostage. He runs down the stairs and through*
> *the auditorium,* BEN *and* JUSTIN *in hot pursuit.*
> *There is a brief beat of uncomfortable silence on stage.*
> SIMON *begins to tip-toe off, leaving* TRISH *and* PATSY.]

TRISH   *(improvising, in character)* Strange. I wonder ... what is to become of us. Or what ... in fact has transpired ... to bring us to this ...pretty pass?

PATSY   *(improvising, in character)* I'll bet me rudder, this scoundrel here, *(indicating* SIMON*)* can blow the fog from that question.

SIMON   *(having not made it off)* I'm too bloody old for this, Patsy. My nerves...

PATSY   Stow yer blubbering and tell us how it is you an' yer evil twin Antonio came ta' dump such a cargo a grief on these poor players.

TRISH   Brave Patsy, I believe the Maestro here is merely a puppet, in the hands of his fiendish brother.

PATSY   I catches yer drift. It were his evil twin all along, a'course. Antonio, posing as yourself. This tale grows more twisted than a jib in a hurricane. Am I right?

SIMON   What? Oh yes, absolutely.

PATSY   Chained you in his dungeon, did he?

SIMON   What? No...or possibly. Yes, it's coming back now. Chained? Oh yes. *(showing his wrists, pained)* Ouuuu! Ah!

PATSY   Why?

SIMON	What?
PATSY	Why did he chain you in his dungeon?
SIMON	Oh yes. Ah? *(looking to* TRISH*)*
TRISH	So he wouldn't…tell?
SIMON	Oh yes, that's right. Couldn't tell. No. Mustn't tell.
PATSY	Tell what?
SIMON	About the um…the big…the very large… um?
TRISH	*(top of her head)* Marriage?
SIMON	Yes! That's it. Marriage. *Hugely* married.
PATSY	Who?
SIMON	*(pointing to* TRISH*)* She. That is, her and I. Married. Secretly, of course.
PATSY	Any babbies?
SIMON {	Not really.
TRISH {	Just the one.
SIMON	*(an explanation of their discrepancy)* Just a *tiny* one.
PATSY	Tiny babbie?
SIMON	Um, yes.
PATSY	And?
SIMON	And…um…gone?
PATSY	Gone?
SIMON	Um… Sold her … in fact.
PATSY	To…?
SIMON	um…well…You know ehheheheheheh black market…babbie buyers.
TRISH	Pirates.
SIMON	Yes, pirates, actually. Strange. Full circle, really.
PATSY	You say this girl child was tiny? Do you mean… short?
SIMON	Well it was a babbie/baby? Right darling? Short baby? Um…could be. Yes.
PATSY	*(indicating)* Did she have a half-moon birth mark on her neck? Like this!
SIMON	Um … ?
TRISH	Yes!
PATSY	*(throwing her arms out)* Father! Mother!
SIMON & TRISH	Patsy! Patsy child.

[*They embrace. A door opens suddenly in the auditorium.* CLAIRE *runs in,* BEN *behind her.* BEN *is without his weapon and the scalpel is embedded in his arm. Blood.*]

CLAIRE He's hurt.

BEN I'm fine.

[JUSTIN *enters next, backed into the room by* ANTONY *who has* BEN's *sword and seems to be winning.*]

ANTONY Do you know, a little blood-letting has really cleared my head.

[BEN *pulls the scalpel from his arm.* ANTONY *and* JUSTIN *parry and thrust with fierce determination, up on to the stage.* TRISH *pulls* BEN *aside and rips a piece from the hem of her skirt to tie off* BEN's *bleeding arm.*]

ANTONY Play's over, darling.

[ANTONY *slices over* JUSTIN's *head causing him to duck.*]

ANTONY Take a bow.

[ANTONY *punches* JUSTIN *in the face, causing him to fall on the "little stage." He moves in for the kill. Before he can deliver the* coup de grace PATSY *pricks* ANTONY *in the behind with her sword.*]

PATSY Yer poop's exposed, ya barnacle.

ANTONY Tiny Talent Time.

PATSY Have at you! *(goes at him)* Harr! Harr! *(*PATSY *is disarmed)* Help! *(then, as she retreats)* A horse! A horse! My kingdom for a horse!

[PATSY *runs around and under the staircase.* ANTONY *begins to chase* PATSY *but is tripped by* JUSTIN. ANTONY *does a fierce double-sword flourish then engages* JUSTIN. PATSY *emerges, running out from under the other side of the staircase.* JUSTIN *and* ANTONY *fence on the floor, then the staircase.* JUSTIN *is driven backwards.* ANTONY *manages to disarm* JUSTIN. *The sword falls down to the stage floor.*]

ANTONY Let's make a stab at that closing tableau shall we?!

[BEN *rushes to pick up the sword.* ANTONY *pushes*

JUSTIN *out the inn door.*]

BEN   Put up your blade, Antonio!

ANTONY   Fool!

[BEN *runs up the stairs and engages* ANTONY. *They thrust and parry down the stairs and eventually onto the stage.* ANTONY *and* BEN *drive* CLAIRE, PATSY, TRISH, *and* SIMON *downstage left.* BEN *manages to get one sword away from* ANTONY. BEN *tosses the sword to* JUSTIN.]

ANTONY   Well, that's it, boy. You're definitely not asked back!

[*All three fence spectacularly.* ANTONY *wounds* JUSTIN *in the leg — not seriously, but enough to disable him, and yanks* BEN *around, disarms him, and shoves his head into the iron bars of the stair railing.* ANTONY *tosses* BEN*'s sword off stage right.* ANTONY *and* JUSTIN *swash stage left.* ANTONY *slashes at* JUSTIN, *who jumps out of the way at the last second, and* TRISH *sits on the blade.* ANTONY *is unable to pull it free.*]

ANTONY   Shove off, you great cow.

[PATSY *has grabbed a large prop basket of fruit and begins hucking fruit at* ANTONY.]

ANTONY   Infernal pigmy!

[ANTONY *begins to chase* PATSY.]

ANTONY   Come here! Keep your place!

[CAROL *enters, still dressed as pirate, downstage right just as* PATSY *and* ANTONY *are heading towards it.* PATSY *throws the basket to* CAROL *and keeps running.* ANTONY *passes* CAROL, *still hot after* PATSY. JUSTIN *tries to free* BEN *from the railings.* TRISH, *realizing she has the sword, hot potatoes it to* SIMON, *who tosses it to* CLAIRE, *who tosses it offstage.* ANTONY *emerges, running, from under the stairs, having caught* PATSY (*dummy*). *He struggles with her. Her hands are at his throat. He whirls her around and eventually tosses her at* CAROL, *who is standing directly in front of the gate door holding the basket.* PATSY (*dummy*), CAROL, *and the basket all fall backwards through the door. They lie there stunned.* JUSTIN *manages to pop* BEN*'s head*

back out of the railings. JUSTIN *tosses sword to* BEN.
BEN *advances on* ANTONY. ANTONY *runs behind the
wicker basket then lifts the lid to shield* BEN'*s thrust.*
BEN'*s sword sticks in the lid.* ANTONY *grabs a
tambourine from the basket and whacks* BEN *across
the side of the head, disarming him, and at the same
time forcing him into the basket.* ANTONY *locks the
basket. He then takes the sword ánd stabs it into the
basket.* CLAIRE *does a dance move across the stage,
and kicks* ANTONY *in the head. She then grabs his
sword, and, twirling across the stage, does a big finish.*
ANTONY *cracks his head back into alignment.*

ANTONY Meddling bunhead!

[CLAIRE *tosses the sword offstage.*]

ANTONY Traitors! Turncoats!

[JUSTIN *moves towards* ANTONY.]

JUSTIN *(exhausted)* Antony, stop. Stop this.

ANTONY But lovee, I'm a deranged evil twin. It's what I do.

[ANTONY *begins to strangle* JUSTIN. PATSY *and* CAROL
charge on from stage right. PATSY *seems to be sitting in
a basket that is carried by* CAROL. *This is all done by
one actor.* PATSY'*s top half (head arms, torso) is real,
her legs are false.* CAROL'*s top half (head, shoulders,
arms, etc. to the waist) are false. The bottom half
(skirt, legs, shoes) is real.* PATSY *has on a Greek helmet,
holds a Greek spear in jousting position, and is playing
*BEN'*s Indian horn from* The Raj *like a battle trumpet.*

PATSY Pa, pa pa pa pa pa!

[PATSY *and* CAROL *overshoot their mark.* CAROL *runs
right across the stage and the spear becomes imbedded
in the stage left proscenium arch.* PATSY *is occupied
trying to pull it out. She doesn't succeed.* TRISH *rushes
to pull* ANTONY *off of* JUSTIN. ANTONY *rebuffs her
and drags* JUSTIN *to the little stage to finish strangling
him.* TRISH *runs to the skiff and releases* BEN. BEN *gets
out, tangled in a large period shirt, which he hands to
*TRISH. BEN *dives on* ANTONY *and pulls him off of
*JUSTIN. *They roll about, each trying to gain the upper*

hand.]

ANTONY   We should really strip down and do this proper.

[JUSTIN *winds up and socks* ANTONY *in the jaw.* BEN *and* TRISH *have positioned the period shirt so that* ANTONY's *arms slide into the sleeves, working like a straightjacket.* JUSTIN *stuffs* ANTONY's *mouth with a prop and they all drag him to the curtain upright on the little stage.* PATSY/CAROL, *seeing things are in hand, signals the booth for a music cue and then exits. The cast pull ribbons out from the top of the upright. Music cue begins. The cast maypole* ANTONY *to the upright. Music ends.*]

JUSTIN   *(back to the text of* The Twins*)* Go, wretch! Go! And never again cast your tyrannical eyes on this troupe of players! Go!

CLAIRE   Giro, fierce pirate, what think you of your Orazio now? *(off with moustache, hat, letting down her hair)* Or rather your Beatrice. For yours I truly am, if you would have me. *(They kiss.)*

TRISH   I pray someone unfold this tale, for surely 'tis stranger than most upon our stage, and would lack all credit had I myself not played a role.

JUSTIN   The churlish poet whom this chaos penned
Is Fortune sure. Now Fortune makes amends
By writing each an ending that begins
New life, new love. New fortunes with... the Twins

[CLAIRE *as Beatrice, and* JUSTIN *as Giro, kiss.* TRISH *as Lucille, and* BEN *as Orazio, kiss.* JUSTIN *steps forward.*]

Epilogue *(spoken by* JUSTIN *directly to audience)*

JUSTIN   I hope, my friends, we have not asked too much of you this night
T'attend there, silent, in the dark while we play in the light.
Imperfect players we confess. Our poet, quite contrite.
Yet I must ask you one thing more before we say

goodnight:
Pray summon up now if you will, the play time of your
youth:
Young limb, sweet song, a childhood game,
adventures impromptu.
When play was natural as breath. When play was
given due.
When all pretend, and all far-fetched was simple to
make true.

But some of us in growing up, have lost, or set adrift,
Or given up, forgot, or worse; been beaten from that
"gift"
By tyrant brutal. Bully cold. Who threats to punish swift
Any and all who dare to play and celebrate that gift.

Now if by chance you find yourself oppressed in some
employ,
We pray you'll not forget the gift no bully can destroy.
For play is more than childhood game, much more
than fancy's toy.
It is a way to find a way, to heal, release, bring joy.
   [*as* JULIA]
And if, in some slight measure, we have pleased you
with our play,
(begins removing her beard and moustache)
Then grant this humble player the more pleasure back
to say:
To please you is our best reward. To play for you our
bliss.
For sans your presence here tonight, our play is
emptiness.
   [*The cast onstage react to seeing that it is* JULIA. *The
   cast bow.* TRISH *and* SIMON *come together.* BEN *and*
   JULIA *come together. The two couples kiss. All celebrate
   as the curtain descends.*]

THE END

A Short History of the Ibsen Festival

The Ibsen Festival began as the shared dream of the people of Oslo, Ontario. In the early sixties, hard times hit and our beloved Hastverk Fish Pickling Plant (specializing in herring and smelt) went under. Undaunted, the city fathers vowed to save the town and dared to dream.

Although Oslo had no previous connection whatsoever to Scandinavian culture (apart from its name, of course), a Jungian collective dream experienced simultaneously by the entire populace inspired the first Summer Festival of Norwegian Culture in 1961. Nordic dancing demonstrations, folksong concerts, Norwegian potlucks, Fouggenborky-ball tournaments, and fast-fillet contests abounded, but at the heart of our celebration was our community players' production of *A Doll's House*. So successful was this thespian endeavour (standing ovations both nights) that the town fathers decided to follow in the footsteps of Ontario's other festival towns. Our architects and town planners donated their services to "Norwegianize" the town and evoke a mid-nineteenth-century ambience. Local businesses came on board, adopting Ibsenesque names: Hedda Hair (hair salon); Gabbler's Pub; Ghosts Funeral Parlor; Gynt Pier Inn; The Doll's House (souvenirs and "Home of the Denterbuster" Norwegian Fudge with nuts); Wild Duck (gourmet dining); Master Builder (contracting and plumbing — "we specialize in saunas"); Enemy of the People (fumigating and pest control); Little Eyeolf (optometrist); J.G. Borkman's

Men's Wear; Lady from the Sea (swimwear and ladies' summer fashion).

The town's shared dream was well on the way to becoming a reality.

In January 1962 the abandoned Hastverk Fish Pickling Plant was converted into a theatre, and in April the entire Oslo Town Council formed the search party which set out for England to find an artistic director. Desmond Bentley-Butt ("Buttey") was chosen for his firm hand, reputation as a taskmaster, and unabashed love of the colonies. Under Mr Bentley-Butt, our first season — starring three of the great regional British stars of the day as well as a few Canadians with festival experience — was a great success.

After five seasons the "Ibfest" moved into our current complex, which houses the Festival Stage and our second space, The Red Herring, which is devoted to our winter murder mystery series for local audiences.

Buttey remained in Oslo for five seasons. When he resigned under mysterious circumstances, he handed over the mantle to his great chum and countryman, Roger Smithe Peake. Peake put Oslo on the international map with his policy of hiring only international actors. Canadian actors were, of course, welcome at the festival, but only after serving five years or more in another country. These were heady times. *Hedda Gabbler on Ice*, the puppet production of *A Doll's House*, *The Nude John Gabriel Borkman* ...

Then followed a string of "unstable" artistic directors:

- The Ibfest ushered in its tenth season with a new artistic director, Lawrence Leslie Alcock. Mr Alcock was with the festival for only one season. He fled back to London after being charged by the Oslo vice squad with "lewd behaviour in a public place."

- Terrence Derik Dullich, who programmed a season of six productions of *Ghosts*, was let go after his first season.

- Philip Sedgewick, who insisted on designing all productions himself, flooded the theatre with one thousand tonnes of sand for a production of *Lady from the Sea*. The stage floor gave way and the theatre was closed for three months, cutting short the season and Sedgewick's career.

- Cecil Breen-Buteal, a lovely man from London, was made to step down after insisting the entire company convert to Catholicism. Buteal remained in Oslo for the summer, abducting astonished tourists and baptising them against their will.

- Caroll Channing — not *thee* Carol Channing, but rather a very high-strung British gentleman — was driven mad by the acting company, who would hum songs from *Hello Dolly* just under its breath.

- Trevor Napier-Arden-Jones — "Emma" to his friends — was recommended very highly by all sources in London, but it seems he had never directed before arriving in Oslo. Nevertheless, Emma gained popularity as a great jokester and bon vivant. He disliked rehearsal and admitted loathing all things theatrical. Emma brought over scores of "chums" to direct for him and was well-liked in the community, but vanished just before the late opener.

Antony Manley-Dunn was hired by Emma to direct the late opener, and stayed on for twenty-one years. Since his arrival our town has grown to embrace millions of theatregoers who swarm to the Ibfest from around the world. Oslo the town has become synonymous with Ibsen the festival, and we are delighted that you are part of our dream come true. Whatever your taste in theatre, you're sure to find something to enjoy at the Ibsen Festival!

Play Synopses

The Twins
by Oro Silverati

A brilliant but little-known playwright, Silverati was to Goldoni what Ben Jonson was to Shakespeare. *The Twins* is considered his *magnum opus*, largely because it is the only piece of work in his canon which he actually managed to complete, and because it is the first documented Italian example of the theatrical device of a play within a play.

In this moving but comic gem, the Rasponi twins, Beatrice and Orazio, leave home together to seek their fortune but are separated in a shipwreck. Alone in the world, Beatrice disguises herself as her brother. "He" is rescued by pirates, who sell him to Maestro Spavento, a tyrant who owns a Commedia troupe in which Beatrice is forced to perform. Romance abounds, gender confounds, and it really does turn into a comedy of errors. Lots of laughs, *lazzi*, and *burle*, and the occasional *concetti*.

Virtue Slandered
by William Weatherby

One of the great classics, *Virtue Slandered* is truly a gem of the Restoration period. Adultery and acquisitive sexuality are at the heart of the play. The dialogue speaks with wit, and true to the spirit of comedy, the play ends with an imminent marriage, even though the institution itself has taken an incredible battering at the hands of the playwright. Weatherby, one of the three famed "Williams" writing at the time, is said to have snarled at a dog that bit him, "I wish you were married and living in the country."

Virtue Slandered traces the antics of Lady Valentine and Lady Lustford, cousins who aid one another in their separate intrigues. Lady Valentine has a mysterious secret admirer with whom she has a "literary relationship." Lady Lustford and her husband, Sir Insatiable, are in constant turmoil, taunting one another with their many interludes. Cuckolds, conquests, and confetti — *Virtue Slandered* is a cornucopia of comedy.

The Raj
by Gottal and Spitalfields

The Raj marks the pinnacle of the collaboration of the famous nineteenth-century playwright, Gottal, and the equally famous composer, Spitalfields. Since its opening at the Savoy Opera in 1885, *The Raj* has been delighting audiences around the world and has been translated into 32 languages. As in all G&S's work, mockery and music mask the pessimistic assumptions that manners and politeness serve only to hide fundamental human selfishness.

The Raj takes a light but satirical look at well-meaning British Imperialists in colonial India. Colonel Clive and his homesick wife, Lucinda, love, laugh, and sing their way through adventures with the "quaint natives." The sentiments of the most-loved number in the show are perhaps best summed up by the character of Sadoom: "Memsahib, for all your Western wisdom, there are some things you don't know."

Pantilous in Crete
by Cretinus

Cretinus was one of the most admired poets of Old Comedy, and *Pantilous in Crete* is the only tragedy attributed to him. It has been a huge point, hotly debated throughout the ages, whether or not this play came about as a result of Aristophanes' challenging Cretinus to "write something serious for a change." This incident is said to have occurred when the two rival playwrights had comedies billed back-to-back at the City Dionysia Festival in 455 B.C.

Aristotelian in structure, *Pantilous in Crete* chronicles the downfall of its tragic hero because of *hubris*. Having offended Zeus, Pantilous is doomed to a life of horror and grief and is bound for eternity to a stone column. His sister Hermineyers and nephew Deadus are also hapless victims of Zeus's ire, albeit in an indirect way. **WARNING:** Although events on the tragic stage never include violence, some may find the messenger's descriptions of decapitation and eye-gouging dangerously graphic.

Frozen Wheat
by Gerry Green

This Canadian classic, which premiered in 1964, shocked audiences to the core but thrilled critics from coast to coast. With this, his first play, Green was immediately heralded as Canada's answer to Edward Albee. *Frozen Wheat* was the first in Green's cycle of seven domestic plays which use land images as metaphors for our national and regional identities and cultural conflicts. Next season we will be mounting *The Elm Tree Dieth*, the second instalment of his renowned cycle.

Frozen Wheat is a beautifully drawn portrait of the Bédard family. Alphonse and his wife, Sylvie, a Québécois couple stranded on the prairies in the dead of winter, have to come to terms with their son's growing up "Anglais," their daughter's teenage pregnancy, and a surprise visit from their hard-drinking East Coast relatives. Hard-hitting but humorous, this touching exploration of country and family is profoundly moving.

Olaf Liljekrans
by Henrik Ibsen
Translated by Brenda Van Staffelburg

This early masterpiece has seen only two previous productions: its premiere at the Norwegian Theatre in 1857, and an apparently very unfortunate staging at the Rehearsal Theatre in London in 1911. *Olaf Liljekrans* marks the end of Ibsen's early Romantic nationalist period. The original idea for the play was drawn from the folk tale *The Grouse in Justedal* and the epic *Ballad of Olaf,* which Ibsen fused to achieve a unique stylistic vacillation between ballad, saga, and "modern" realism. For further context, a copy of Ibsen's essay "The Heroic Ballad and its Significance for Artistic Poetry" can be purchased at The Doll's House Gift Shop adjacent to our theatre lobby.

    Olaf Liljekrans opens with the old minstrel Thorgejr listening to the first chorus, sung by Lady Kirsten's household, exhorting Christians to awake from their enchantment. What follows is an intricate love triangle where Olaf must remain true to his heart, as opposed to the financial needs of his noble family. Eventually Olaf vows to marry his true love Alfhid and live on the mountain until the time comes to ride to heaven on the angels' wings.

Tom Wood is an accomplished playwright, actor, and director. He has worked with every major regional theatre in Canada and has spent seven years with the Stratford Festival and five with the Shaw Festival.

Claptrap is Wood's third play. His first play, *North Shore Live*, written with Nicola Cavendish and Bob Baker, is a satire about television. The play won Vancouver's Jessie award for Best New Play, and after a successful run in Vancouver enjoyed a national tour. Mr Wood's second play, *B-Movie: The Play*, is a farce about our obsession with movies. *B-Movie* won five Dora Mavor Moore awards and the Chalmers Award for Best New Play. *B-Movie* originated at the Phoenix Theatre, Edmonton, and was then moved to Toronto by the Shaw Festival, where it ran to sold out houses at the Toronto Workshop Productions. The subsequent year it was re-mounted by Centre Stage and broke all box office records for a Canadian non-musical run.

Ms Patricia Nye
C/O: Christopher Banks and Associates
Suite 610
6 Adelaide Street, Toronto, Ontario
M5C 1H6
Tel: (416) 214-1155

Front cover illustration, "The Monster Arrives," by Ken Garnhum. Used by permission of the artist.
Back cover photographs by Gordon King Photography. Used by permission.
    Lisa Horner as Louise; Janet Wright as Sylvie; Caleb Marshall as Claude; Roger Honeywell as Gary Wolfe, in "Frozen Wheat."
    Lisa Horner as Mouthpiece; Tom Wood as Monsieur Foppington Lushlace, in "Virtue Slandered."
    Caleb Marshall as Deadus; Roger Honeywell as Pantilous; Janet Wright as Hermineyers, in "Pantilous in Crete."
    Roger Honeywell as Colonel Clive; Janet Wright as Lucinda, in "The Raj."
    Set and costume design by Leslie Frankish.
Endnotes researched and edited by Iris Turcott.

Printed in the USA
CPSIA information can be obtained
at www.ICGtesting.com
JSHW012055140824
68134JS00035B/3459